True Stories of
Teens in the Holocaust

SHATTERED YOUTH IN NAZI GERMANY

PRIMARY SOURCES FROM THE HOLOCAUST

Other Titles in the
True Stories of
Teens in the Holocaust
Series

COURAGEOUS TEEN RESISTERS
PRIMARY SOURCES FROM THE HOLOCAUST
ISBN-13: 978-0-7660-3269-9

ESCAPE—TEENS ON THE RUN
PRIMARY SOURCES FROM THE HOLOCAUST
ISBN-13: 978-0-7660-3270-5

HIDDEN TEENS,
HIDDEN LIVES
PRIMARY SOURCES FROM THE HOLOCAUST
ISBN-13: 978-0-7660-3271-2

TRAPPED—YOUTH IN THE
NAZI GHETTOS
PRIMARY SOURCES FROM THE HOLOCAUST
ISBN-13: 978-0-7660-3272-9

YOUTH DESTROYED—THE NAZI CAMPS
PRIMARY SOURCES FROM THE HOLOCAUST
ISBN-13: 978-0-7660-3273-6

True Stories of
Teens in the Holocaust

SHATTERED YOUTH IN NAZI GERMANY

PRIMARY SOURCES FROM THE HOLOCAUST

Linda Jacobs Altman

Holocaust research by
Margaret Shannon,
Senior Research Historian,
Washington Historical Research

Enslow Publishers, Inc.
40 Industrial Road
Box 398
Berkeley Heights, NJ 07922
USA
http://www.enslow.com

Library of Congress Cataloging-in-Publication Data

Altman, Linda Jacobs, 1943–
    Shattered youth in Nazi Germany : primary sources from the Holocaust / Linda Jacobs Altman.
        p. cm. — (True stories of teens in the Holocaust)
    Includes bibliographical references and index.
    Summary: "Examines the lives of children and teens living in Germany before and during the Holocaust, including the rise of Nazism, growing persecution of Jews, and the Hitler Youth"—Provided by publisher.
        ISBN-13: 978-0-7660-3268-2
        ISBN-10: 0-7660-3268-X
        1. National socialism and youth—Juvenile literature. 2. Jewish children in the Holocaust—Germany—Juvenile literature. 3. Hitler Youth—Juvenile literature. 4. Germany—Politics and government—1933–1945—Juvenile literature. I. Title.
        D804.5.C45A48 2010
        940.53'180835—dc22   2008048002

Printed in the United States of America

092009 Lake Book Manufacturing, Inc., Melrose Park, IL

10 9 8 7 6 5 4 3 2 1

Every effort has been made to locate all copyright holders of material used in this book. If any errors or omissions have occurred, please contact us at www.enslow.com. We will try to make corrections in future editions.

☘ Enslow Publishers, Inc., is committed to printing our books on recycled paper. The paper in every book contains 10% to 30% post-consumer waste (PCW). The cover board on the outside of each book contains 100% PCW. Our goal is to do our part to help young people and the environment too!

To Our Readers: We have done our best to make sure all Internet addresses in this book were active and appropriate when we went to press. However, the author and the publisher have no control over and assume no liability for the material available on those Internet sites or on other Web sites they may link to. Any comments or suggestions can be sent by e-mail to comments@enslow.com or to the address on the back cover.

Illustration Credits: Courtesy of the Arnold-Liebster Foundation, p. 80; Enslow Publishers, Inc., p. 49; Courtesy of Jurgen Herbst, p. 77; Rue des Archives / The Granger Collection, New York, pp. 1, 3; ullstein bild / The Granger Collection, p. 105; USHMM, pp. 9, 18, 31, 64, 66, 68, 84, 97, 115, 116; USHMM, courtesy of Annemarie and Waltraud Kusserow, p. 82; USHMM, courtesy of Elizabeth Koenig Kaufmann, pp. 22, 24–25, 115; USHMM, courtesy of Fritz Gluckstein, p. 40; USHMM, courtesy of Hans Levi, p. 21; USHMM, courtesy of Jizchak Schwersenz, pp. 57, 116; USHMM, courtesy of Joe Yablon, p. 113; USHMM, courtesy of Leo Goldberger, p. 47; USHMM, courtesy of Morris Rosen, p. 8; USHMM, courtesy of National Archives and Records Administration, pp. 11, 14, 16, 50, 54–55, 115; USHMM, courtesy of Ralph Harpuder, p. 35; USHMM, courtesy of Richard Freimark, p. 73; USHMM, courtesy of Roland Klemig, p. 89; USHMM, courtesy of Ruth Levine, pp. 28, 115; USHMM, courtesy of William O. McWorkman, pp. 92–93; USHMM, courtesy of Yad Vashem, p. 111.

Cover Illustration: Rue des Archives / The Granger Collection, New York (The face of a thirteen-year-old Hitler Youth member captured by American soldiers in 1945).

Contents

Acknowledgments

Special thanks to the people of the United States Holocaust Memorial Museum in Washington, D.C., for all their help in completing this book.

Chapter One

THE TEENAGE ASSASSIN

By the autumn of 1938, Nazi Germany was just waiting for an excuse to strike a decisive blow against the Jews. The wait ended when a Jewish teenager in Paris unwittingly gave them exactly what they wanted.

On November 7, Herschel Grynszpan walked into the German Embassy and asked to speak to an official. When the receptionist asked the nature of his business, Grynszpan would only say that it was urgent and of a personal nature. The clerk directed him to Ernst vom Rath, the only attaché available at the time.

Once inside vom Rath's office, Grynszpan took out a gun and fired at point-blank range: once, twice . . . perhaps five times. Gravely wounded, vom Rath stumbled to the doorway and called for help. Two men ran toward him. While they tended the fallen diplomat, his seventeen-year-old assassin waited quietly, almost as if he wanted to be arrested.

He never denied that he went into the embassy to shoot somebody, claiming that he acted "in the name of 12,000 persecuted Jews."[1] Those Jews were Polish citizens who had been living in Germany, some for many years. Under Adolf Hitler, their lives had become perilous, but they hung on as best they could, hoping their situation would improve. In October 1938, they ran out of time.

Nazi troops snatched Jews from their homes, packed them into trains like so much cargo, and dumped them at the Polish border.

Herschel Grynszpan assassinated Ernst vom Rath on November 7, 1938. This portrait was taken of Grynszpan after his arrest by French authorities.

In this wasteland between two nations, there was never enough food to go around. They lived in makeshift dwellings, without decent sanitary facilities. Worse yet, there seemed to be no end to their suffering. Germany would not take them back, and Poland would not let them in.

Herschel Grynszpan's family was among these trapped Jews. After he received a letter from his sister describing their plight,

Grynszpan could think of little else. The family's misery and his own powerlessness gnawed at him day and night, until he hit upon the plan that would take him to the German Embassy by way of a Paris gun shop.

Nazi Propaganda

While Ernst vom Rath fought for his life in a Paris hospital, the Nazis churned out propaganda. The headline of every German newspaper screamed the news: A German diplomat had been shot by a Jewish assassin. The stories appeared on the morning of November 8. By that evening, angry Germans roamed the streets, harassing every Jew they could find.

The Nazi propaganda chief, Joseph Goebbels, exploited this anger, using every available resource to whip up strong anti-Jewish feelings. By the evening of November 9, the uproar was like a cache of dynamite waiting for a fuse to set it off. The fuse arrived at 9:00 P.M., when sources in Paris reported vom Rath's death.

Reinhard Heydrich, the "blond beast" as he was often called, stepped into

Nazi propaganda chief Joseph Goebbels used the assassination of vom Rath to stir up anti-Jewish sentiment among angry Germans.

the picture. Heydrich knew how to stir up hatred and play on the weaknesses of others. These abilities served him well when he set out to organize what would become known as *Kristallnacht*. He wanted the outbreak to appear completely spontaneous—random acts of outrage against a people whose very existence threatened the German nation.

Mobs raged through German cities and towns, setting fire to synagogues, smashing windows, destroying Jewish property, and brutalizing Jewish people. The shattered glass of shop windows lay in mounds on the sidewalks, hence the name *Kristallnacht*, or the Night of Broken Glass. According to Reinhard Heydrich, the violence of November 9 and 10 left 7,500 businesses destroyed, saw 267 synagogues burned to the ground, and resulted in the deaths of 92 Jews.[2]

> Mobs raged through German cities and towns, setting fire to synagogues . . . and brutalizing Jewish people.

After the horror and violence of Kristallnacht, the Nazis had about 25,000 Jewish men arrested and then sent them to concentration camps. Most were released about two weeks later, but the Nazis had made their point: The Jewish community as a whole would be punished for the acts of one member.

Beginning the Holocaust

Herschel Grynszpan faded from public view along with headlines about the assassination. The boy himself was incarcerated at the Fresnes juvenile prison in Paris. After Germany conquered France in 1940, Grynszpan fell into Nazi hands. From that time on, the

Germans pass by a broken shop window of a Jewish-owned business that was destroyed during Kristallnacht. The beginning of the Holocaust is often traced back to the Night of Broken Glass.

trail goes cold. The Germans passed up the good chance for a well-publicized show trial followed by a dramatic execution. There is no record of any trial at all, nor does Grynszpan's name show up in prison records after 1940. He was probably executed quietly, soon after his transfer to Germany.

Many historians trace the beginning of the Holocaust back to Kristallnacht. Using the act of a desperate teenager as an excuse, the Nazis launched nationwide violence against the Jews. Burning synagogues and smashed windows stunned the world, terrified Jewish communities, and previewed the murderous fury that would soon descend on the Jews of Europe.

Chapter Two

THE NAZI RACIAL STATE BEGINS

Germany's Nazi era began on January 30, 1933, when President Paul von Hindenburg appointed Adolf Hitler to the office of chancellor. However, President von Hindenburg did not want to give the second-highest position in the national government to a man he neither liked nor trusted. He considered Hitler little more than a thug with a knack for rabble-rousing.[1]

Hitler was a high school dropout with a spotty work record, but he knew how to sway the masses. With rallies, parades, and fiery speeches, he transformed the Nazi Party from an unknown extremist group into a national force. The term *Nazi* is a nickname, drawn from the first word of the party's full name: National Socialist German Workers' Party.

The Nazi party based its political philosophy on extreme nationalism, racism, and authoritarianism. Hitler governed Nazi Germany as an all-powerful dictator whose smallest word had the force of law.

He promised a glorious future in which a German "master race" would forge the greatest empire the world had ever seen. War was the price of building that empire. Genocide—the systematic killing of entire racial, cultural, or religious groups—was the price of perfecting the "Aryan" race, which is what Hitler called the Germanic and Nordic peoples.

Reichspräsident von Hindenburg und Reichskanzler Adolf Hitler begrüßen sich am 21. 3. 33 in Potsdam.

Adolf Hitler shaking hands with President Paul von Hindenburg on March 21, 1933. Von Hindenburg and his advisors underestimated Hitler's leadership power.

Von Hindenburg's advisors knew about Hitler's extremism, but they thought they could control him. Let Hitler be the public face of government, they said. Let him rally the masses with his pomp and pageantry. But behind the scenes, vice-chancellor Franz von Papen would be in charge.

The advisors soon realized they had made a terrible mistake. Nobody could control Hitler. From the first moment he became chancellor, he began transforming Germany into a Nazi state.

Chancellor Hitler

On the night of Adolf Hitler's appointment, Nazis throughout Germany celebrated with torchlight parades. In the capital city of Berlin, thousands of brown-uniformed storm troopers, as the Nazi militiamen were often called, marched past the chancellery. Hitler stood on the balcony, taking their stiff-armed Nazi salute.

For Gentile, or non-Jewish, teenager Melita Maschmann, the procession was a life-changing event. More than thirty years later, she wrote that

> some of the uncanny feel of that night remains with me even today. The crashing tread of the feet, the somber pomp of the red and black flags, the flickering light from the torches on the faces and the songs with melodies that were at once aggressive and sentimental.
>
> For hours the columns marched by. . . . I longed to hurl myself into this current, to be submerged and borne along by it. . . . At one point somebody suddenly leaped from the ranks of the marchers and struck a man who had been standing only a few paces away from us. Perhaps he had made a hostile remark. I saw him fall to the ground with blood streaming down his face and I heard him cry out. . . . The image of him haunted me for days.
>
> The horror it inspired in me was . . . spiced with an intoxicating joy. "For the flag we are ready to die," the torch-bearers had sung.[2]

For Melita Maschmann, joy won out over horror. She went on to become a loyal Nazi and a leader in the League of German Girls, or *Bund Deutscher Mädchen* (BDM).

That same night, a rabbi's son in the town of Gross-Strehlitz ended up marching in a torchlight parade. Ezra BenGershôm was

President Paul von Hindenburg, standing in window, watches a torchlight parade outside of the chancellery the night Hitler became chancellor of Germany on January 30, 1933.

eleven years old when his class was invited to take part in a huge community celebration:

> When I arrived at school . . . the pupils were already formed up in columns, class by class, and were preparing to march through the town behind their teachers. I quickly got into line and, like all the others, had a torch thrust into my hand.
>
> I was not sure what we were celebrating. . . . I was 11 years old and it gave me enormous pleasure not to be an onlooker for once but actually to be taking part in the procession. . . . [They] were even letting

us march in step behind a military band, holding blazing torches in our hands.

As we reached the more brightly lit streets of the town centre, I noticed that the procession included . . . Hitler Youth and SA [storm trooper] detachments. The "military band" turned out to be a regular SA formation. What was going on? . . . It was not until long after that memorable evening that I realized the truth: our torchlight procession had been to celebrate Hitler's appointment as chancellor.[3]

Building the Racial State

Racism and antisemitism, or hatred of Jews, were part of Nazism from the beginning. The Nazis killed Poles, Russians, and Gypsies because Hitler considered them to be "subhuman." They also killed infants with birth defects, people with mental illness or mental retardation, and those who had simply grown too old to be considered "useful" in the new Germany.

In addition to killing these people, the Nazis sterilized thousands, often without their knowledge or consent. In building their German "master race," they wanted to be sure that people with genetic defects could not have children. They also sterilized many people whose only so-called defect was part-African ancestry.

Mixed-race children faced a hard life in Hitler's Germany. Hans Massaquoi experienced these hardships firsthand. A son of a German mother and an African father, Hans was only seven years old when Hitler came to power. At first, Hans celebrated with his friends. Not until a year later did he realize the danger he was in:

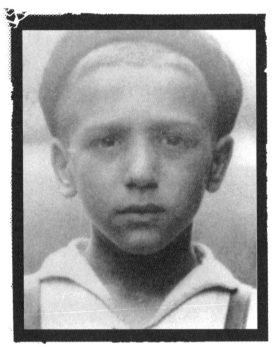

Ezra BenGershôm, eleven years old when Adolf Hitler became chancellor, marched in a torch-light procession with his class.

Once Hitler was firmly in control of the nation, there . . . was never a dull moment in Hamburg. Each week brought new major events and excitement. . . . There were endless processions of SS, SA, and Hitler Youth units marching through the city to . . . the fighting marches of the Nazi movement, dramatic torchlight parades at night, and fireworks over the [lake]. None of these events . . . [seemed to present] any . . . personal threat until the . . . early part of 1934, when I was in the third grade. On that particular day . . . I got my first inkling of the danger the Nazi regime might pose for me.

It was a bizarre twist of fate that the newly formed local Nazi chapter chose for its weekly meeting place Zanoletti's tavern and meeting hall, [next] to the apartment building in which we lived. For several months, our new neighbors and I were obliv-ious to each other's existence. . . . Then the inevitable occurred. It happened on a beautiful spring Sunday that had started

. . . with a [Nazi] parade through our neighborhood. . . . [It] . . . had attracted large crowds of spectators, who were lining the parade route. . . . I watched until the last unit of storm troopers had marched by and the crowd started to disperse.

As I walked home, I heard loud singing and shouting coming from the building next to ours. . . . I tried to catch a glimpse through the wide open door of Zanoletti's meeting hall. It was packed [with] . . . brownshirts. . . . None of them seemed to notice me. . . . Or so I thought. Suddenly, I felt myself grabbed from behind by two huge fists and lifted into the air. . . . I stretched and bent . . . like a fish on a hook. The next thing I knew, I had slipped from the grip of the two fists and was running as fast as I could. . . . I might have made good my escape had it not been for two other Brownshirts who . . . blocked my path. Like a hawk descending on his prey, the SA trooper reclaimed his hapless quarry and this time, none of my kicking, wiggling, and biting could loosen his viselike grip. . . . The SA trooper was about to lift me to the speaker's platform, apparently as an exhibit of . . . racial defilement when he found himself confronted by an enraged woman who was staring at him with hate-filled eyes. . . . Momentarily startled by this trembling, yet apparently fearless woman, the giant SA trooper loosened his grip. Before . . . anyone . . . could comprehend what was taking place, I was once again snatched and dragged through

```
the carousing throng, but this time by my
mother, who hauled me off to the relative
safety of our home.⁴
```

Hitler and the Jews

Of all the targeted groups, Hitler reserved his deepest hatred for the Jews. He said they were like vermin and called upon good Germans to make their country, and eventually all of Europe, *Judenfrei*, or free of Jews. In pursuit of this goal, the Nazis stripped Germany's Jews of their livelihood, their citizenship, and even their right to live. Later they did the same to Jews in the countries they occupied during the war.

The official persecution of Jews began with a one-day boycott of Jewish businesses on April 1, 1933. Uniformed storm troopers stood outside of Jewish businesses, telling people not to go inside. In Willy Schumann's hometown, there was one Jewish family. They owned the Haus T., a clothing store for men and boys.

Gentiles, including Willy and his family, shopped at the store regularly:

```
My parents liked . . . the high quality of
the merchandise and the reasonable prices.
. . . I remember the time my mother and I
went to Haus T. to purchase a pair of short
pants for me. . . . As we approached the
store we saw two young SA troopers in their
yellowish-brown uniforms, high black riding
boots, and peaked caps with chin straps in
place. They had posted themselves to the
left and right of the main entrance and
were holding writing pads and pencils
in their hands, quite obviously for the
```

The Central Committee for the Defense against Jewish Atrocities and the [Jewish] Boycott issued this public notice on April 1, 1933, instructing Germans to boycott all Jewish businesses for one day.

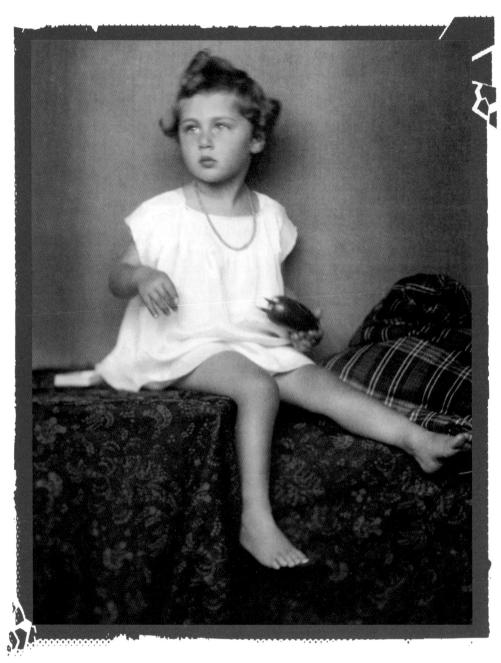

This studio portrait of Elizabeth Kaufmann (now Koenig) was taken in 1927. Her family had to flee Berlin because of Nazi persecution.

```
purpose of writing down the names of all
customers entering the store. My mother
hesitated briefly but then went in anyway,
and we were not harassed by the SA men.
The brightly lighted main business room was
completely empty. Frau T. herself served
us. When my mother asked a question about
the lack of customers, she replied . . .
"Nobody comes in anymore," and then she
cried. On our way home, my mother was very
quiet. After she had told my father about
our experience, I remember that the mood in
our house was of depression, and probably
fear. It was the last time that any of my
family went shopping in the Haus T.5
```

Other anti-Jewish actions in 1933 included the Law for the Reestablishment of the Professional Civil Service, which began removing Jews from government jobs. The Law Concerning Admission to the Legal Profession placed restrictions on Jewish lawyers and judges. Still, other laws put quotas on college admissions for Jewish students and restricted Jews from participating in the arts, owning land, and being newspaper editors.

This last prohibition changed the lives of Elizabeth Koenig and her family. Elizabeth's father was a very well-known journalist in Austria:

```
At that time [when Hitler became chancellor],
my father had moved his family; my brother,
myself, and my mother to Berlin, and when
the Nazis came to power, we lived [in the
city]. He [Koenig's father] was very . . .
endangered because he was . . . on the Nazi
```

```
blacklist as a liberal writer
and journalist.
    I didn't know [about the
blacklist] at the time. My
parents didn't tell me. . . .
I only knew that we packed
in a hurry and left Berlin
as soon as possible which was
easy for us because we had
Austrian passports. . . . My
father had lost his job. And
so . . . our life became very
restricted from that time on.⁶
```

Eleven-year-old Edith Reimer also found her life greatly restricted by the Nazis. To her, Hitler's coming to power "was the end of a happy, carefree childhood; a process of fast maturing began."⁷

Lost Adolescence

Thousands of Jewish young people had to grow up fast. The rise of Nazism overshadowed their lives. Lore Metzger was twelve years old when her "joyous, happy childhood changed . . . with unbelievable speed after Hitler's rise to power." She remembered that

```
[signs] bearing such menacing messages
as "Jews are forbidden to enter here,"
appeared at the entrances of the swimming
pool, the theaters, the parks, the movies,
the zoo and all the restaurants.
    Jewish homes were soiled with swastikas,
the Nazi insignia, and hateful anti-Jewish
```

The rise of Nazism destroyed childhood for thousands of Germans. After fleeing Berlin, Elizabeth Koenig and her family ended up in France. She drew this picture in her sketchbook during her stay in Nazi-occupied France in the early 1940s. The drawing is titled, "Elizabeth and her mother arrested by French gendarmes."

slogans. Organizations informed their Jewish members that their presence was no longer permitted. . . . [Every] so often, Jewish men as well as children were beaten up in the streets and over and over again we heard of smashed-in windows on our beautiful synagogue, or of overturned tombstones in the Jewish cemetery.[8]

Carola Stern Steinhardt was not yet a teenager when Hitler came to power. She did not understand why her Gentile friends abandoned her:

> I had lots of German friends . . . sometimes one of my friends would go with me to synagogue, and I went with her to church. My mother told me I shouldn't kneel down because that's not in my religion, so I didn't. Nobody bothered, I don't even think they did kneel down. . . . But, I went to church Sundays and [my friend] went to synagogue on Saturdays. We were really close friends. . . . But it changed in 1933. It changed a lot. . . . This particular friend didn't change too much, but I had one girl which really was my idol. She was extremely intelligent, and she was a little redhead and she was very cute. And we played together, and at one point she said to me, "You know, Carola, I can't play with you anymore." And I said, "How come?" She said, "Because you're a Jew." I said, "What is that?" She said, "Well have you heard of Hitler?" I . . . said yes . . . because every morning they used to say Heil Hitler. "But why can't you play with me anymore? Why?" She said, "Because my father told me that you're Jewish, and . . . Aryan kids can no longer play with the Jewish kids." . . . Then suddenly . . . the whole group [of non-Jewish friends] disappeared. Nobody would play with a Jewish child anymore. So then we were all Jewish kids, and we stuck to one another.[9]

Jews became fearful of going to synagogue or participating in Jewish religious rites and celebrations. In a later oral interview, survivor Walter F. recalled his Bar Mitzvah, a rite of passage in which a boy assumes the religious and spiritual responsibilities of an adult:

> I was supposed to be bar mitzvahed in 1933, in June shortly after [I became] thirteen, but that was right after the seizure of power by the Nazis, and things were very unsettled. Everybody was nervous, what are we going to do, [are] we going to bar mitzvah or not bar mitzvah, and a bar mitzvah normally was a big affair. Normally my bar mitzvah would have been an affair of 500 people, 1000 people I don't know what. Family from all over, from Mannheim, from Darmstadt, from Bebra, from Kassel, from Eisenach, so what are we going to do, we're not going to have a big bar mitzvah. Maybe we're not going to have a bar mitzvah at all. Finally they, my parents, decided we were going to have my bar mitzvah in January 1934, which was about seven or eight months later. And that bar mitzvah was very small. There were maybe 30 people. Twenty-nine Jews . . . one non-Jew. That man represented the Gestapo [secret police]. He was in the temple. They wanted to make sure the rabbi didn't say anything offensive.[10]

In some cases, the realization of change came from a small event rather than a major one. For Alfred Feldman, it came from "a small, inconspicuous event" in the city of Cologne:

27

The rise of Nazism quickly changed Jewish life in Germany. The Bar Mitzvah of Walter F. went from a large event to a very small gathering watched by the Gestapo in 1933. This portrait shows another boy, Josef Radzinski, having his Bar Mitzvah. In 1942, Radzinski was deported to Treblinka, a Nazi death camp in Poland.

I had arranged to meet Aunt Betty in a public square. . . . When I arrived, she was not alone. A woman walked alongside the baby carriage, berating my aunt for having sat on a public bench. Aunt Betty angrily countered that she paid her taxes and had as much right to sit there as anyone else. The woman left in a huff, and we observed that, having reached the far side of the square, she talked to a policeman. Aunt Betty thought it prudent to leave the square.

As we passed a newsstand, she showed me . . . an issue of *Der Stürmer* [an anti-semitic newspaper] . . . its bold headlines proclaiming some outrage committed by Jews, caricatured there with large noses, devious eyes, and hairy profiles evoking the face of sheep.

Within me, feelings of indignation welled up at the malice, the insult, the calumny [false charges] of the thing. It evoked a sense of being snubbed, of having been chastened [punished] that was not without fear.[11]

When President Paul von Hindenburg died on August 2, 1934, Hitler stood ready to do what he believed had to be done. He had already stripped the *Reichstag*, or the parliament of Germany, of its power to make laws. With von Hindenburg dead, Hitler made the next move: claiming the presidency for himself and combining it with the chancellorship. Thus, he became Führer and Reich Chancellor, the supreme leader of the German nation.

After Hitler became supreme leader, he increased the pace of his Nazification campaign. By September 15, 1935, he had enacted the Nuremberg Laws, which—among other things—stripped Jews of their German citizenship and outlawed marriages between Jews and "Aryans."

Excluding Jews

Henry Landman was fifteen years old when the Nuremberg Laws went into effect. Later, he recalled the impact on his family and friends:

> With one single stroke of the pen, my family lost its German citizenship. All Jews, even those listed as "quarter Jews," were deprived of their status as citizens and relegated to "subjects" of the State. We could not marry outside our own faith.
>
> Slowly and deliberately, we lost all status within the German State. In time, we would not even be allowed to buy food from the same store as an Aryan. . . . The Nuremberg Laws wiped out any . . . sense of equality that we may have [held]. We were stripped of our rights and, in time, our property. . . .
>
> In 1938, Heinrich Himmler, the powerful head of the SS [Nazi special security

force] made the Jews sell their land and possessions to the Germans—at a lower price. We were forced to take our valuables to a . . . city clerk, who dutifully and efficiently gave you a receipt. No one on either side of that desk . . . expected to see those valuables ever again; but you had to go through the sham transaction.

By September 15, 1935, Hitler had enacted the Nuremberg Laws, stripping Jews of many citizenship rights. This photo shows Hitler saluting his followers at a rally.

There was no choice. By involving the
German citizens as recipients of the Jewish
jewelry, lands, and factories, the Third
Reich guaranteed the cooperation of the
Germans themselves, since they would get
the profits of the lower sale price.

By 1938, no Jew could ride a train, go to restaurants with
Gentiles, nor attend classes. Even driver's licenses were revoked.
By official decree, all Jewish males took on the extra name of
"Israel" on their documents. Women also had to add "Sara" to
each of their documents.[1]

Identifying Jews and Enemies of the State

The Nuremberg Laws led to disputes over who was—and who
was not—to be considered a Jew. On November 14, 1935,
the Nazis added a new decree to clarify any questions of Jewish
identity:

Partly Jewish is anyone who is descended
from one or two grandparents who are fully
Jewish by race. . . . A grandparent is
to be considered as fully Jewish if he
belonged to the Jewish religious community.
. . . A [full] Jew is he who is descended
from at least three grandparents who are
fully Jewish by race. . . .
   Only the Reich citizen, as bearer of full
political rights, exercises the right to
vote in political affairs, and can hold
a public office. . . . A Jew cannot be a
citizen of the Reich. He has no right to
vote in political affairs, he cannot occupy
a public office.[2]

In order to enforce antisemitic laws, Nazi authorities wanted to recognize Jews immediately and under all circumstances. Starting on October 5, 1938, Jewish passports had to be stamped with a red "J" for *Jude*. On September 1, 1941, Jews had to begin wearing big Jewish stars on their clothes. As Dora Kramen Dimitro, a Jewish survivor said: "We wore yellow stars so they should know who is a Jew, and we walked on the street too, not on the sidewalk. . . . This was different because they had to know that we are Jewish."[3]

Another addition to the Nazi race laws dealt with Jewish names, requiring Jews to have recognizably Jewish first names: "Insofar as Jews have given names other than those which they are permitted to bear . . . they are required as from January 1, 1939, to take an additional given name; males will take the given name Israel, females the given name Sara . . . "[4]

The Threat Grows

Easier identification led to greater persecution. One teenager recalled how the growing danger forced his family to seek an escape:

> There was a young man whom we knew from the swimming pool and when it was still open to Jews we would go swimming there, my brother and I, and one time, a young fellow about our age started beating us up and if we had really resisted that would have made it worse. . . . [There were many things] that we couldn't do anymore. There were many places where you couldn't go on vacation anymore. These were mild things, but being beaten up at the swimming pool, I felt it

was getting worse and worse. My parents
[thought so] as well, and so in 1936 . . .
they made serious efforts to contact our
relatives in St. Louis in order to try
getting us out.[5]

In addition to suffering from random violence, more Jews
were arrested by the Gestapo, a secret police division of the SS.
Eve Nussbaum Soumerai recalled her terror one autumn day in
1937, when her father went out on an errand and did not return:

On . . . Sunday . . . Papa disappeared. He
had left his brother Max, who was making
arrangements to leave for Shanghai via
Italy, and was on his way home. . . . Mama
sat by the window till it got dark. I could
hear her muffled sobs during the night. . . .
Papa's "comrade" attorney Johann von
Ledersteger, who also owned our apartment,
promised Mama he would do all he could to
locate Papa, whom he supposed had been in a
roundup. "Berthold," he said, "received the
Iron Cross . . . that should help."
  I was devastated. My father, my best
friend, was gone. . . . After ten long
weeks, Papa returned with his belongings
in a cardboard box tied with string. . . .
[everyone] listened intently to what had
happened to him in . . . prison. "The food
was terrible: watery soup and stale bread.
But we had cards, played Skat, and told
funny stories." It sounded like a vacation
in Switzerland. We had done all the suffering, or so it seemed. That night when Papa
once again sat on my bed, I challenged him
and came straight to the point. "We missed

All Jewish passports had to be stamped with a red "J" by October 1938.

you. We were afraid. Mama cried all night.
I suffered too." I was a little vague as
to how I had suffered. Papa was silent.
"Didn't you miss us? Weren't you sad? How
could you enjoy yourself like you said you
did?"

After a long silence, Papa said, "Evchen,
this might be difficult for you to understand, but it is possible to play cards,
tell jokes, laugh, and be frightened all at
the same time. You laugh and feel like cry-
ing. But when you laugh, you make others
laugh. And suddenly there is hope. You feel
the energy of laughter and friendship. And
most important, you become the leader. You
stand tall. And you know what, you will
make a dent in setting things right. It's
your form of resistance. Sorrow, outrage,
infinite sadness, yes, tears, too, are ever
present, but you are in charge, in charge
of your laughter and your sorrow. Remember
that always." And he tucked me in tighter
than usual and left the door ajar so that I
could see the light in the living room.[6]

Jews were not the only ones singled out by the Nazis. Roma
and Sinti, often referred to as Gypsies, and people of African
heritage were considered racially inferior to Aryans. Others were
marked because of their religious beliefs, sexual orientation, or
political opinions.

Edith Gerder Reimer remembered the fate of one non-Jewish
classmate:

Her father was a member of the Communist
Party. Rather than live under the Nazis,
he decided to kill his entire family.

Evidently he had discussed this dramatic
action with his wife. The day before the
murder-suicide the girl came to class
as usual, but during a short recess, she
suddenly . . . announced quite gaily, that
[she would] not be in school the next day,
because her father was going to kill the
whole family, [including] herself. . . .
Not one of us took her seriously; I doubt
that she, herself, was fully aware of the
tragedy.[7]

Spreading the Reich

Identifying and isolating Jews played an important role when
Germany annexed new territories. In 1938, Austria became part
of the new German Reich. It happened quickly without a single
shot being fired. When German troops marched into Vienna, the
capital, on March 12, crowds of cheering Austrians greeted them.

Jewish young people soon found their world turned upside
down: friends deserted them, schools expelled them, strangers
accosted them in the streets. Anti-Jewish measures plunged their
families into poverty. Before the annexation, about 192,000 Jews
lived in Austria, and Vienna was an important center of Jewish
culture and education. But by December 1939, only 57,000 Jews
remained. Many had fled the country.

In October 1938, the Nazis took over the Sudetenland region
of Czechoslovakia. Once more, Hitler took the territory without
fighting for it, and again, more antisemitic measures followed.
Magda Lipner remembered that her

happy life changed suddenly after 1938. . . .
The Germans marched in [triumphantly]. . . .

   A few months later my father lost his
permit to operate our shipping and moving
co. He did continue work illegally and
[got] many fines. We lost our financial
security. We haven't had enough income. My
father started to sell different items at
home. Like cooking oil. . . . My father
didn't have enough money . . . he borrowed
from his second cousin, and he gave as
collateral a small diamond pendant. I
found this out only after the war, when
he returned it to me.[8]

Kristallnacht: Berlin

On the night of November 9, 1938, after Herschel Grynszpan had
shot and killed a German diplomat in Paris, France, the Nazis saw
a chance to use this against the Jewish community. They staged
violent demonstrations and claimed that they were spontaneous
acts of revenge by outraged German citizens. Rioters burned
synagogues and destroyed Jewish-owned shops. They smashed so
many windows that broken glass lay like snowdrifts on the sidewalks, giving the rampage its name. Ernest Fontheim, a Jewish
high school student, saw horrors that he would never forget:

Thursday, November 10, 1938, started like
any other day, I left our apartment on
Kaiserdamm in the West end section of
Berlin at around 7:20 for the nearest rapid
transit . . . a half-mile walk past apartment buildings and one-family villas. There
were no signs of any unusual activities.

From there I took the train for a 15-minute ride to the Tiergarten Station in central Berlin near the high school of the orthodox congregation Adass Yisroel where I arrived a few minutes before the beginning of the school day at 8 o'clock. When I entered my classroom, some of my classmates were telling horror stories of what they had seen on their way to school like smashed store windows of Jewish-owned shops, looting mobs, and even burning synagogues. A fair number of students [were] absent. The 8 o'clock bell rang signaling the beginning of classes, but no teachers were in sight either in our class or in any of the other classes along our corridor. That had never happened before. I don't remember anymore how long it took for the teachers to emerge from the teacher's conference room [but it] finally opened and the teachers streamed out to their various class rooms, they all looked extremely grim.

"... some of my classmates were telling horror stories of what they had seen on their way to school like smashed store windows ..."

When our teacher Dr. Wollheim entered the room and closed the door, all talking stopped instantly, and there was complete silence in the class. That too was unique, for in general we were a fairly undisciplined bunch, and it usually took several admonitions until some quiet was established. In a tense voice Dr. Wollheim announced

39

that school was being dismissed because our safety could not be guaranteed. This was followed by a number of instructions which he urged us to follow in every detail. Number one, we should go home directly and as fast as possible without lingering anywhere or visiting friends so that our parents would know that we are safe. Number two, we should not walk in large groups because that would attract attention and possible violence by hostile crowds. He concluded by saying that there would be no school for

After Kristallnacht, beginning in 1939, Nazi laws also forced Jews over the age of ten to wear a Jewish Star of David on the outside of their clothing to identify them as Jews.

the foreseeable future and that we would be notified when school would reopen again.

I quickly walked back to the Tiergarten Station and decided to look out the window when the elevated train would pass the Synagogue Fasanenstrasse where I had become Bar Mitzvah. . . . I literally felt my heart fall into my stomach when I saw a thick column of smoke rising out of the center cupola. There was no wind, and the column seemed to stand motionless reaching into the heavens. At that moment all rationality left me. I got off the train at the next stop and raced back the few blocks as if pulled by an irresistible force. I did not think of Dr. Wollheim's instruction nor of any possible danger to myself. Police barricades kept a crowd of onlookers on the opposite sidewalk. Firefighters were hosing down adjacent buildings. The air was filled with the acrid smell of smoke. I was wedged in the middle of a hostile crowd which was in an ugly mood shouting anti-Semitic slogans. I was completely hypnotized by the burning synagogue and was totally oblivious to any possible danger. I thought of the many times I had attended services there and listened to the sermons all of which had fortified my soul during the difficult years of persecution. Even almost six years of Nazi rule had not prepared me for such an experience.

Suddenly someone shouted that a Jewish family was living on the ground floor of the apartment building across the street from the synagogue. Watching the fire, the crowd was backed against the building. Someone else shouted: "Let's get them!" Everyone turned around. Those closest surged through the building entrance. I could hear heavy blows against the apartment door. In my imagination I pictured a frightened family hiding in a room as far as possible from the entrance door—hoping and praying that the door would withstand, and I prayed with them. I vividly remember the crashing violent noise of splintering wood followed by deadly silence, then suddenly wild cries of triumph. An elderly bald-headed man was brutally pushed through the crowd while fists rained down on him from all sides accompanied by anti-Semitic epithets. His face was bloodied. One single man in the crowd shouted: "How cowardly! So many against one!" He was immediately attacked by others. After the elderly Jew had been pushed to the curb, a police car appeared mysteriously; he was put in and driven off. I left this scene of horror completely drained . . . and went home. . . . What has remained and will forever remain in my memory is the image of the thick column of smoke standing on top of the center cupola of that beautiful synagogue and the bloodied bald head of an unknown Jew.[9]

An Orphanage in Dinslaken

The violence of Kristallnacht was not limited to Berlin. It spread to cities and towns all over Germany. When the news reached an orphanage in the town of Dinslaken, director Y. S. Hertz had to curb his own fears in order to help the children:

> I forced myself not to show any sign of emotion. Only thus could I avoid a state of panic among the children and tutors. . . . About 7:30 A.M. I ordered 46 people, among them 32 children, into the dining hall of the institution and [made a] brief address: "As you know, last night . . . a member of the German Embassy in Paris, was assassinated. The Jews are held responsible for this murder. . . . during the next few hours there will certainly be anti-Semitic excesses. . . . Nobody will remain in the rooms of the upper floor of the building. The exit door to the street will be opened only by myself! From this moment on everyone is to heed my orders only!"
>
> At 9:30 A.M. the bell at the main gate rang persistently. I opened the door: about 50 men stormed into the house. . . . At first they rushed into the dining room, which fortunately was empty, and there they began their work of destruction. . . . The frightened and fearful cries of the children resounded through the building. In a [loud] voice I shouted: "Children, go out into the street immediately!" . . . The children immediately ran down a small

"I vividly remember the crashing violent noise of splintering wood followed by deadly silence . . ."

staircase at the back. . . . We tried to reach . . . Dinslaken's Town Hall, where I intended to ask for police protection. . . . the senior police officer, Freihahn, shouted . . . "Jews do not get protection from us!" . . . . Freihahn then drove all of us to the wet lawn of the orphanage garden. He gave us strict orders not to leave the place under any circumstances.

Facing the back of the building, we were able to watch how everything in the house was being systematically destroyed. . . . we could hear the crunching of glass or the hammering against wood as windows and doors were broken. Books, chairs, beds, tables, linen, chests, parts of a piano, a radiogram, and maps were thrown through [openings] in the wall, which a short while ago had been windows or doors.

"We could hear the crunching of glass or the hammering against wood as windows and doors were broken."

At 10:15 A.M. we heard the wailing of sirens! We noticed a heavy cloud of smoke billowing upward. It was obvious from the direction it was coming from that the Nazis had set the synagogue on fire. Very soon we saw smoke-clouds rising up, mixed with sparks of fire. Later I noticed that some Jewish houses, close to the synagogue, had also been set alight under the expert guidance of the fire-brigade. Its presence was a necessity, since the firemen had to save

the homes of the non-Jewish neighborhood.
. . . Nobody was allowed to leave the
[orphanage yard].

Men considered physically fit were called
for duty. Only those over 60, among them
people of 75 years of age, were allowed to
stay. Very soon we learned that the entire
Jewish male population under 60 had already
been transferred to the concentration camp
at Dachau.

I learned very soon from a policeman,
who in his heart was still an anti-Nazi,
that most of the Jewish men had been beaten
up by [storm troopers] before being trans-
ported to Dachau. They were kicked, slapped
in the face, and subjected to all sorts of
humiliation.[10]

A Narrow Escape

The events of Kristallnacht unfolded without rhyme or reason;
some people were killed, some imprisoned and beaten. For no
particular reason, some escaped the worst. Eve Nussbaum
Soumerai and her family were among the lucky ones:

In the afternoon of November 10th, without
explanation, our teacher dismissed the
class early, asking us to go straight home.
. . . None of [us] asked why—we were happy
to go home early.

When I got off the streetcar on
Wallensteinstrasse and walked the half-
block toward our apartment house, I got
the first inkling that this was to be an
extraordinary day: the inside of the shul
[synagogue] on the ground floor of the

apartment house was being destroyed. Men were axing the benches and other furnishings. I walked up a flight of stairs and saw a physician's apartment being destroyed— furniture and chandelier. I was frightened. I continued up one more flight and rang the bell to our apartment. My mother ushered me in quickly and motioned me to be quiet. The shades to all our windows were drawn. Soon my brother Norbert, who had celebrated his Bar Mitzvah 13 months earlier, came home from school. My parents then discussed a strategy for dealing with the Nazis, who, according to my parents, were sure to pay us a call . . . [and] would be looking for money and other valuables. My parents mainly [worried] about . . . two bank books [for accounts containing] the funds we needed [for] passage to the United States. We expected to [go] in December, when our quota numbers for the American visas were due to come up. . . . My mother sewed the . . . bank books . . . into [our pajama tops]. . . . My brother and I went to bed early, as my parents hoped that the Nazis would neither disturb the children nor dis- cover the bank books. My mother prepared 30 marks in cash to turn over when they asked for money. My parents stayed up and waited.

   [The Nazis] came at 11 o'clock. . . . I was fully awake, but pretended to be asleep. They asked for money and my mother gave them the 30 marks. They then searched all the rooms, including the room my brother and I were in, and took all the jewelry and silverware they could find. . . . They did

Many synagogues were burned down or destroyed during
Kristallnacht. This photo shows a synagogue in Opava, a city in
the Sudetenland region (present-day Czech Republic), during the
November 9 and 10 destruction.

not disturb us children and did not find the bank books.

Finally before they left, I heard them ask my father to put on his coat—he was to go with them. . . . My father pleaded that he had never done anything wrong and that an Austrian colleague of his who had been a long-standing member of the Nazi party would vouch for him. . . . At long last, the men left—miraculously without my father.

The next day we learned that my father was the only adult male resident of the apartment house who had been spared; all the other men, about 20, had been taken away—to Dachau. . . . By the time we left . . . for the United States . . . the men had not returned.[11]

A Best Friend

Kristallnacht was a turning point for Eve Nussbaum Soumerai. It represented the end of a lifelong friendship:

Best friends, true friends, are a necessity your whole life, whether you are young or old. Best friends listen to your secrets and worries and are always there to help you. You never need to tell them a lie because they are on your side and understand everything.

Adelheid was my very best friend. Our mothers met when they were carrying us in their respective stomachs. Adelheid believed that we had met in another life because we were so close and knew each

This map shows the many cities in Germany and surrounding regions where synagogues were destroyed during Kristallnacht. Countless amounts of Jewish property were damaged and thousands of Jewish men were arrested.

other so well that we did not even have
to talk. . . . Our mothers were also
friends. They shared recipes, books, and
secrets.[12]

Adelheid began to change after she joined the *Bund Deutscher
Mädchen* (BDM):

She loved going to meetings and told me
on a few occasions how much fun they were.
We were still talking but she started to
inject bits of awful news, such as she had
heard that Mama's favorite author Stefan
Zweig's books were burned in a big fire,

A torchlight procession around a bonfire of "un-German" books on
May 10, 1933. Eve Nussbaum Soumerai learned about the burning
of "un-German" books from her "Aryan" friend Adelheid. Their
friendship ended shortly after Kristallnacht.

and that's when I knew for sure she had begun to hate me.[13]

Shortly after Kristallnacht, Adelheid came to Eve's house:

I was alone when the doorbell rang. Adelheid, in full uniform, stood outside. . . . Without a greeting of any kind, she demanded that I hand over all the photos taken of us together since we were babies. I was unable to move.

"You know where they are, hurry up," she said. When I still did not move, she added, "They are in that cigar box in the bottom draw of your [dresser], in case you forgot." Was it my imagination or was she sneering? "Get them or I will." That did it. I ran to my room while she stayed at the door. A minute later I came back with the cigar box in which I kept my photos and spilled the contents on the floor. Photos of Adelheid and me as babies mixed in with those of my family greeted us, smiling. There was one of our first day of school, each of us carrying one of those large, decorated cones filled with goodies and licking chocolate lollipops. . . . Adelheid knelt down, tore the photos into many pieces, spilled them on the floor, and yelled, "You people are like rats," and left running.

I picked up the bits of photos, put them back into the cigar box, and locked myself in my room and cried until I had no tears left. Her words had devastated me. We had been best friends ever since we were babies. What happened? We were rats?

How can you change from best friend to a
rat? These questions have pre-occupied me
for most of my life. On this day they came
into sharp focus.[14]

From personal tragedies like a shattered friendship to assaults on whole Jewish communities, Kristallnacht was a turning point. Many Jews who had not planned to leave Germany decided that emigration was their only hope—if only a safe haven could be found. Unfortunately, the few safe havens that existed were open to only a relatively small number of Jews. As Germany moved toward war, Jews who could not escape found themselves trapped by the Nazis, who wanted to destroy them.

Chapter Four

JEWS AND OTHER NON-ARYANS AT NAZIFIED SCHOOLS

Nazification, the process of imposing Nazi standards and ideals on German society, began as soon as Hitler came to power. Because Hitler had a special interest in Nazifying young people, schools were among the first targets: "I begin with the young," he once said. "We older ones are used up. We are rotten to the marrow. . . . But my magnificent youngsters! Are there any finer ones in the world? Look at these young men and boys! What material! With them, I can make a new world."[1]

The Nazification process brought young people face-to-face with a new order that favored propaganda over education and imposed its racial policies on both students and faculty. Like life in general, life at school was divided into before and after Hitler.

The Problems Begin

In most schools, the first evidence of change was the so-called "Hitler salute." According to survivor Henry Landman:

> It became a law of the school that you had
> to salute every teacher with the new, but
> now well known, salute of the extended hand
> and open palm. "Heil Hitler" would be said
> with a stern and proud voice as you passed
> a senior faculty member. In time, more and
> more faculty would wear a uniform and the
> corridors were loud with the sounds of

"Heil Hitler!" . . . .
This would tear through
me; I would [shudder]
every time that I heard
it; I would feel sick when
I had to say it. Hearing
the salute would make me
realize that I was truly
an outsider . . . in the
country of my birth![2]

For Simone Arnold Liebster, the salute became a special problem. She was a Jehovah's Witness; saluting the Nazi flag or saying "Heil Hitler" was against her religion. Despite persecution, she would not conform to the Nazi ideology of hate. This put her at odds with the Nazis:

[Every morning], the whole
class got up. During the
singing of the national
anthem, *Deutschland über
alles*, the *Horst-Wessel-Lied*, and other
Nazi songs, everyone had to salute with
arms outstretched. Mr. Ehrlich ran around
with his ruler hitting any child whose arm
started drooping. My arm never went up in
spite of the physical reminder. The whole
class was terrorized. [The teacher] ordered
me: "You'll not leave my class until you
write the words of each song ten times!"
But the clock ran out. Escaping the morning
ordeal, the children ran out as fast as
they could. I stayed behind, but he sent

The Vienna Boys Choir giving the "Hitler salute." It became a law in
German schools that all children must salute their teachers.

me out. I went down slowly and very
[fearfully]. Outside they waited for me.
Mr. Ehrlich opened the window to watch with
satisfaction as peer pressure came down on
me. Mute and frightened, I faced the other
children. They stared at me. Finally, a
voice said, "Keep resisting that swine!"
All repeated, "Resist, resist." Upstairs
the window slammed shut. I still had no
words.[3]

Acts of resistance rarely found this kind of support. This was especially true for Jewish students like Walter F.:

> [After] Hitler [came to power] . . . they
> started school with the teacher coming in
> and everyone jumping up and [saying] "Heil
> Hitler!" . . . Of course you didn't want
> to be left out so everyone raised his hand,
> including myself. . . . We had . . . one
> teacher who was teaching biology, chemis-
> try, and physics . . . Dr. B. He was an old
> Nazi . . . [that meant] someone who joined
> the Nazi party back in the early 1920s. As
> a result he wore not just a swastika but a
> swastika in gold. This was a big deal for
> those guys. . . . he was teaching [genet-
> ics], dominant and recessive genes and all
> that. . . . he [taught that] all the reces-
> sive genes were in the Jews, and the Jews
> were bad. . . . [He] was always giving me a
> bad grade. That's the only time I ever got
> a 3-, you know 1 was for best, 5 was for
> the worst grade, 3- was pretty bad from my
> point of view. I was always at least a 2+
> sort of student. [Dr. B] was the only one
> I was . . . having . . . troubles with.
> . . . [Still], I left high school because
> either that or they would tell me to get
> out. . . . they were trying to get rid of
> Jewish students.[4]

Mistreating Jews and Other Non-Aryans

Early attempts to get rid of Jews and other non-Aryans focused on making them want to leave. This meant making their lives very miserable in classes and excluding them from extracurricular activities. For Gad Beck, the pressure began in earnest when his school was renamed to honor a fallen Hitler youth. Beck never forgot the ceremony that made the name change official:

> [E]verybody had to go out in the school-
> yard. I went too. "No, no," the teacher
> said, "Not you, stay there." I stayed. A
> minute later he came and took me to the
> schoolyard. And stood me against a wall

This portrait shows Gerhard (Gad) Beck (right) and his sister Margot (Miriam). Gad Beck saw many changes in his school that attempted to outcast Jews and non-Aryans.

across from the rest of the pupils. They all stood with their faces to one side, and I stood here, and there were 12 others with me. We were all the Jews in the school. I didn't know that. Except for two or three that I knew because I went to religion classes with them. I didn't know them, and now we stood there and we stood there, and the flags were being raised, the German flag, the Nazi flag, the Hitler Youth flag, and then the songs were sung, and then they raised their arms . . . and from this day on it was the same every morning. They called it the flag raising ceremony. I went home. I cried. And I said to my mother, "I can't do it, I can't do it. . . . What have I done to them?" And [always] the same excuse [from my parents:] "It will pass. Nobody is doing anything to you." Nobody had done anything to me. Very interesting. Nobody had hit me. That wasn't part of the Hitler Youth program. They were supposed to . . . isolate the Jews, but not hit them.[5]

For Ezra BenGershôm, being Jewish had not been a problem until the Nazis arrived:

On the whole, my relationships with the other members of my class were not bad. Nor, at first, did this change when something like two-thirds of them joined the Hitler Youth. What did change . . . was the way in which I was treated by Hitler Youth members in other classes.

One break-time, a first-year started baiting me in the playground. "Saucy little squirt," I told him (he was half a head shorter than me). "I'll show you! Give a second-year cheek, would you? Are you daft or something?" And he duly got his ears boxed.

The first-year became steadily more insolent. I had no alternative but to hit him again. Before long we were surrounded by onlookers. They came running from all over the playground—first-years, second-years, even some fifth-years—and formed a dense ring around us.

Voices were raised. "Come over here! The Jew's bashing up someone smaller than him!" "Hit him! Don't let the Jew walk all over you!" A lanky fellow detached himself from the crowd and tried to trip me up. When I did not fall, someone else grabbed my ankles and threw me to the ground beside the first-year. The crowd howled. The unequal struggle ended only when the bell rang for the end of break. . . . I dragged myself up the steps of the building through a hail of jeers and insults and found my way back to the classroom.[6]

> "I dragged myself up the steps of the building through a hail of jeers and insults . . ."

Nazifying the Curriculum

During the Nazi era, everything schools taught was subject to Nazi approval. In keeping with Hitler's ideas about hardened, tough-as-steel German youth, physical education took a central place in the curriculum. For boys, classes began to seem like basic training for the army.

Academic subjects got pushed aside, and the remaining lessons were weakened because the Nazi administration determined what could and could not be taught. For example, in literature and composition classes, teachers could not use any of the twenty thousand books incinerated in the book burning of May 10, 1933. They could not allow students to express controversial opinions in their compositions.

In history, and especially in science, teachers had to present Nazi ideas as fact. This requirement hit hardest in biology, where racial science became the core of the curriculum. Nazi biology was based on the idea that the Aryan race was superior to all others.

"As a black person in white Nazi Germany, I was highly visible and thus could neither run nor hide . . . "

For example, one particular chart was posted in almost every science classroom in Germany. This chart showed Aryans standing far above groups the Nazis called *Untermenchen*, or subhumans: Jews, Poles, Russians, and Africans.

For Hans Massaquoi, racial science was not just something people learned in school; it directly threatened his existence:

> As a black person in white Nazi Germany, I was highly visible and thus could neither run nor hide, to paraphrase my childhood idol [boxer] Joe Louis. . . . I was forced to develop my own instincts to tell me how best

to survive physically and psychologically in a country consumed by racial arrogance and racial hatred and openly committed to the destruction of all "non-Aryans."[7]

Many Jewish students had to endure the humiliation of being used as object lessons in racial science classes. Generally, this involved choosing a student and pointing out his or her traits that the Nazi Party considered inferior. Henry Landman recalled what happened to one of his classmates:

A teacher, who had been open in his hatred for the Jewish people, ordered one of my friends to the front of the class. Emanuel seemed surprised that he was being singled out in the middle of the biology class. . . . I can see his face today as the teacher started to unravel the secret; my friend's crime was that he "looked Jewish." His features certainly were not those of the blond, blue eyed, demigod that the Third Reich favored; that alone was sufficient for this teacher to bring him in front of the class.

"Do you see this boy, Class?" he asked as he pointed to my friend and turned him around like a display doll. The teacher spoke dispassionately, as if he were holding a glass jar with a specimen in it. . . . "Do you see his big nose, his big ears, his thick glasses? Look at his lips. Look at him. This is what the Jew looks like! He is weak and dirty. I must warn you, for your own safety and health . . . if you see anyone like this, STAY AWAY from him.

Do you hear?" His voice was not raised, but rather matter of fact. The Gentiles in the class stared at Emanuel the way one stared at a freak in the circus. They studied him from every angle as if they were trying to absorb the result for future reference. Some took notes. My friend had no choice but to stand there and wait until the teacher was through with him. . . . Finally, the teacher dismissed him. . . . Emanuel slowly walked back to his seat as all Gentile eyes followed him. None of the Jews could look at him.[8]

The teaching of racism did not stop in the classroom, or even in the Hitler Youth meetings. It made its way into music, movies, and books. For example, a picture book called *Trust No Fox in the Green Meadow and No Jew on His Oath* contained the following passage:

When god the Lord made the World,
He also created the races:
Indians, Negroes, and Chinese
Likewise the Jews, the evil beings.
And [we] too, were also there,
The Germans among the others.
Then he gave to all a portion of the earth,
That it might be cultivated by their labor.
The Jew took no part in that work
But from the very beginning, the devil seized him;
He wished not to work, but only to deceive
He was the ace of liars
Learning quickly and well from
his father the Devil . . .[9]

Teachers and Administrators

Part of Nazifying the schools meant replacing those teachers and administrators who were deemed unreliable with loyal Nazis. This had an immediate effect on student morale as well as education. Ezra BenGershôm wrote about the changes when a well-respected headmaster lost his job:

> "Suddenly the sound of heckling arose from among the massed ranks of pupils."

For some reason, all the staff and pupils were assembled in the hall. Dr. Bergmann [the headmaster] mounted the rostrum [an elevated platform for public speaking] and began to address the school. Suddenly the sound of heckling arose from among the massed ranks of pupils. Shocked people turned to see who had dared to interrupt the headmaster. The face they saw was a new one to the school. It belonged to the young officer in charge of the local Hitler Youth, who had taken a seat in the front row. He now rose to his feet and in front of the whole school ordered the headmaster to leave the rostrum. . . . The unheard-of then occurred: Dr. Bergmann clearly felt obliged to comply with the order of the young man in uniform, whereupon the Hitler Youth leader took his place and announced that the headmaster had been dismissed for unreliability.[10]

In a different school, another non-Aryan boy drew unwelcome attention from a new principal. Herr Heinrich Wriede made no secret of his contempt for Hans Massaquoi's African heritage:

„Die Judennaſe iſt an ihrer Spitze gebogen. Sie ſieht aus wie ein Sechſer..."

This page from *Der Giftpilz* (*The Poisonous Mushroom*), an antisemitic German children's book, shows a Jewish student being forced to point out a "Jewish nose." Many Jewish students were used as objects during lessons in racial science classes.

Herr Wriede came into my life—and I into his—sometime during my second school year. . . . To introduce himself to us, he had the entire student body and faculty assemble in the schoolyard, where . . . he strutted around in high boots and riding breeches like a general inspecting his troops. . . . [He said that] things would be done the Wriede way—if we knew what he meant. Of course we didn't know what he meant, but from the tone of his voice we got a pretty good idea that "the Wriede way" was nothing we'd be particularly crazy about.

As he paraded in front of us, he suddenly spotted me among the ranks of boys, and . . . fixed his hateful gaze on me.

"What I intend to instill in this school is pride in being German boys in a National Socialist German state," he [said] without taking his eyes off me. . . . After Wriede had finished and we returned to class, I couldn't rid myself of the unfamiliar and quite unsettling feeling of having just met a personal enemy, someone who wished me ill.[11]

Teachers who dared to defy the Nazi regime put themselves in danger of being fired, imprisoned, or both. Defiance could be anything from speaking out against the Nazis to being compassionate toward Jewish or other non-Aryan students.

Some teachers attempted to find a middle ground, stopping short of open defiance with actions that could be explained away. For example, Walter F. talked about a teacher who developed an effective method of giving mixed messages:

The teaching of racism went outside the classroom, spilling into pop culture. This is an illustration from the picture book, *Trust No Fox in the Green Meadow and No Jew on His Oath*.

> [A] Nazi . . . named M [was] sitting next
> to me, and we were doing a test, a math
> test. Somewhere during the course of the
> test I was working away . . . and the
> teacher . . . said, "M, don't copy Jewish
> work." . . . M of course doesn't look at
> my paper [anymore,] he looks at his paper.
> After that . . . the teacher called me over
> and said, "You know I didn't want to offend
> you. I wanted to show up this Nazi. . . .
> He's a big Nazi and he has to copy Jewish
> thinking. I didn't want to offend you."[12]

Making Schools *Judenfrei*

As teachers who could not accept the Nazi line quit or were fired, conditions grew worse for Jewish students. Lore Metzger recalled that Jewish students

> were required to sit in a special corner
> of the classroom. During the recreation
> period we [had] to use a special place in
> the school yard in order not to get into
> physical contact with our fellow-students.
>   To have to sit in the so-called Jew
> corner, to have to listen to the most
> degrading remarks and to have to avoid
> all contacts with my classmates, who until
> now had been my friends, made these school
> years a period of torment and agony for me.[13]

On November 15, 1938, the government issued a formal order that banned Jewish students from all public schools. School had become such a horrible trial for Klaus Langer that he welcomed the news:

Hans Massaquoi faced persecution everyday in school because of his African ancestry. This photo, taken February 27, 2001, shows Massaquoi (right) at the United States Holocaust Memorial Museum in Washington, D.C., responding to questions about his experiences growing up in Germany.

I did not realize at first that I no longer
had to attend that awful school, with the
"Heil Hitler" at the beginning and end of
every lesson, [with] the way the teachers
talked. Each day that I didn't have to
attend school, I considered myself lucky.
I was not in the least bit sorry.[14]

After banning Jews from German schools, the Reich placed
the responsibility for their education on the local Jewish communities. This became official in an addition to the Nuremberg Laws,
dated July 4, 1939. It broke one of the last links between Jews and
Aryans in Hitler's Germany.

Chapter Five

GENTILE YOUNG PEOPLE: PRESSURE TO CONFORM

While Jewish young people were being forced out of German society, gentile young people were being trapped within it. A steady stream of propaganda told them what to think, what to do, whom to admire, and whom to hate. Hitler made it clear how he thought German young people ought to be trained:

> My program for educating youth is hard. Weakness must be hammered away. In my castles of the Teutonic Order a youth will grow up before which the world will tremble. I want a brutal, domineering, fearless, cruel youth. Youth must be all that. It must bear pain. There must be nothing weak and gentle about it. The free, splendid beast of prey must once again flash from its eyes. . . . That is how I will eradicate thousands of years of human domestication. . . . That is how I will create the New Order.[1]

Education for the "New Order"

This New Order would be based on racism and antisemitism, and would be created through warfare. Nazi education would indoctrinate German youth with the desired attitudes. Even picture books for young children taught hatred and mistrust of Jews. Arithmetic textbooks also helped to indoctrinate a new generation of warriors. For example, one math problem used the following scenario:

> A squadron of 346 bombers drops [fire] bombs on an enemy city. Each aeroplane carries 500 bombs [weighing] 1-1/2 kilograms each. Calculate the total weight of their bomb loads. How many fires will be caused if 30 per cent of the bombs are hits and only 20 per cent of hits cause fires? Day bombers fly up to 280 kilometers an hour, night bombers up to 240. Calculate the flying time from Breslau to Prague.[2]

German Young People and the Hitler Effect

Hitler used his considerable talent as an orator to glorify his plans and begin the Nazification of German life. His power over crowds soon became legendary.

Willy Schumann was eight years old when he first witnessed that power. It happened when Hitler's motorcade stopped briefly in Willy's hometown. People of all ages jostled one another, just hoping for a glimpse of the Nazi leader. In the commotion, Willy saw something he would never forget:

> For the first time in my life I experienced the phenomenon of a "mob" of people. It was a friendly, good-natured, and enthusiastic crowd, but a mob nevertheless. Individuals were no longer in control of their actions and movements. . . . [Hitler] did not make a speech, there was no music, just hundreds of people who had come . . . to wave and cheer [him].[3]

Hitler did not rely upon public appearances to make himself known to the people. Schumann observed that

The Führer was ever-present for all Germans. He was [shown in] newspapers and . . . magazines, in some kind of pose at some activity. When we went to the movies, which at our age at the time had become a ritual, every Sunday afternoon in one of our two local theaters with the admission price of thirty Pfennig, there was always a short film [before] the main feature, sometimes a cartoon . . . [and also] the official newsreel of the week. . . . [which always had] at least one segment showing the Führer "at work." But above all, Hitler's [constant presence] was made possible by the young broadcast medium of radio. . . . Many millions of listeners could be . . . exposed to [an endless] series of mass rallies, parades, harvest festivals, opening ceremonies, memorial day celebrations, state funerals, and, above all, Hitler's speeches. . . .

I have never in my life seen or heard a speaker with more magnetic talent . . . than Hitler; his effect on a mass audience was nothing short of hypnotic. But there was a side effect of my . . . exposure to a master speaker in my formative years. When the Third Reich collapsed and we young people slowly and very gradually began to reorient ourselves, create new values for ourselves, and look for new role models, I made a . . . discovery about myself. I was physically unable to . . . listen to a . . . speech in which the speaker shouts [at the

audience]. . . . This aversion to all noisy
speech making has stayed with me to this
day. . . . I also know that many Germans of
my age-group know and share this feeling.[4]

In telling his personal story, Willy Schumann treats official
antisemitism almost as a nonfactor in his experience with his
opinion:

How did we [young people] react to the
never-ceasing anti-Semitic propaganda in

Adolf Hitler speaking to a massive crowd during Reich Party Day in
September 1935. Hitler's speaking power had a dramatic effect on
Willy Schumann as it did on thousands of young Germans.

```
the news media, in films, textbooks, and .
. . contemporary works of literature? . . .
these attempts at brainwashing were not
effective. The image of "the Jew" remained
strangely vague to us young people.⁵
```

Learning Antisemitism

All German young people had to deal with antisemitism in one way or another. The Nazis flooded Germany with anti-Jewish propaganda. In public, many young people simply parroted what they had heard described as "Jewish evil." In private, some of them struggled with their real feelings and took cues from parents and other family members.

Parental attitudes were important for Melita Maschmann. On her way to becoming an ardent Nazi, Maschmann noted her parents' almost casual antisemitism:

```
As children we had been told fairy stories
which sought to make us believe in witches
                          and wizards. By now we
                          were too grown up to
"By now we were too       take this witchcraft
grown up to take this     seriously, but we still
witchcraft   seriously,   went on believing in
but we still went on      the "wicked Jews." They
                          had never appeared to
believing in the 'wicked  us in bodily form, but
Jews.'"                   it was our daily expe-
                          rience that adults
                          believed in them. After
all, we could not check to see if the earth
was round rather than flat. . . . The
grownups "knew" it and one took over this
```

knowledge without mistrust. They also
"knew" that the Jews were wicked.

For as long as we could remember, the
adults had lived in this contradictory way
with complete unconcern. One was friendly
with individual Jews whom one liked, just
as one was friendly as a Protestant with
individual Catholics. But while it occurred
to nobody to be . . . hostile to the
Catholics, one was [hostile] to the Jews
[as a group]. . . . And when I heard that
the Jews were being driven from their
professions and homes and imprisoned in
ghettos, the points switched automatically
in my mind to steer me around the thought
that such a fate could also overtake [my
Jewish friends]. It was only the Jew who
was being persecuted and "made harmless."[6]

Jurgen Herbst also grappled with the antisemitism he learned
at school and in the Hitler Youth. Years later, he remembered when
his personal struggle began. The day after Kristallnacht, with the
local synagogue still burning, Jurgen rushed home to tell his
mother about it:

I described my walk to school in the
morning, the broken window on the Lange
Herzogstrasse with the half brick lying
among the shoes, the burnt-out synagogue
and the SS motorcycle . . . [the] fires for
which no one would call the firefighters,
and the story about . . . the Morgensterns
on the Bahnhofstrasse. All during the
telling my excitement rose. It had been
such an incredible morning. I had heard

such unbelievable tales. My cheeks were flushed. I felt my ears burn. How could all that have happened and what in the world did it all mean?

My mother, her back still turned toward me and her arms in the hot, soapy water, suddenly straightened up from her dishpan. She turned around slowly and looked me in the face, her arms now hanging straight down at her sides, water and soap bubbles dripping off them and forming puddles on the tiled kitchen floor. And then she said: "Do you know, Jurgen, if you had been Albert Morgenstern, you would have been torn from your bed last night; you, your father, and I would have been pushed down the staircase, and all your toys and books would have been thrown on the street. Had you been born a little Jewish boy, this would have happened to you last night."

I was stunned. I did not know what to think. I could not get the picture out of my mind, the picture of my parents and me being pushed down the stairs. It stayed with me that day as I withdrew into my room to do my school assignments. I tried to read some chapters in my book on German sagas . . . but I could not concentrate. The picture came back, again and again.

It would recur, also, again and again, in the following months and years. It would return unexpectedly and unannounced. It would keep me awake at night, when I lay in my bed, and it would rise before me when, at [Hitler Youth] meetings or in Mr. Fuchtel's class, I would hear more about

Jurgen Herbst was only eleven years old when World War II began. He struggled with the antisemitism he learned in school. This photo was taken of him when he was six years old carrying a bag filled with candy. This was a custom in Germany on the first day of school.

the "Jewish danger.". . . . It became very
clear to me that what happened and what I
had seen had something to do with Jews and
Germans. But exactly what was it that made
Jews so hateful to us Germans? I could not
figure it out.[7]

Inconvenient Truths

When the war turned against Germany, Jurgen Herbst stopped
believing in Hitler's vision of a thousand-year Reich. He kept
most of his thoughts to himself, until one day he finally let his
pent-up feelings spill out:

[It was] on a summer morning in 1944, not
long before our school was closed. . . .
Fear gripped me with jolting intensity. The
air-raid sirens had interrupted our lesson,
we had descended into the basement, and
after the all-clear had sounded we were
waiting in our class-
room for our teacher to
reappear.

"Fear gripped me with jolting intensity. The air-raid sirens had interrupted our lesson, we had descended into the basement . . . "

As we sat idly on
top of our benches,
one of us started it:
"Hermann Goring said
that no British bomber
will ever fly over our
country."

Another added: "Der
Führer said German soldiers do not know the
word retreat."

And soon there was no stopping: "Our
U-boats will totally isolate England." "Our
Africa-Korps will soon join the Arabs in

Jerusalem." "The [swastika flag] will
forever wave over the Caucasus."

So it went, until the words escaped out
of my mouth and I shouted: "This is how
they lie!"

There was an abrupt, absolute stillness.
My eyes fell on one of my classmates, who
happened to be the son of our local SS
chief. As I stared in his face, an ice-cold
hand seemed to brush down my back. What did
I say? What have I done? was all I could
think.

The door opened and our teacher came in.
"You are so quiet this morning," he said
in mock astonishment. Then we turned to our
lesson, and I slowly regained my composure.
Nobody . . . ever mentioned the incident
again.[8]

Simone Arnold Liebster, the Jehovah's Witness who refused to give the "Heil Hitler" salute, did not fare so well. She faced a very painful choice: Give the salute or leave her school forever. The confrontation began with a summons to the principal's office:

I knocked timidly at the door. . . . I
heard "Come in" followed by "Heil Hitler."
My throat tightened. I looked down at
my feet, and I stood motionless in the
doorway.

"Come over here. I'll read you a note
from the city supervisor: "the student Simone
Arnold refuses to salute. It is your duty
to break her resistance or dismiss her from
school." A long silence followed. Mr. Gasser
stood up. He had an impressive stature:

This portrait of Simone Arnold Liebster was taken in June 1943 before she was sent to a re-education home. Simone was expelled from her school after refusing to give the "Heil Hitler" salute.

> "Why do you refuse?" I looked straight into his eyes.
>
> "Because I'm a Christian."
>
> His forehead wrinkled up with surprise, and he said, "So am I."
>
> He picked up the city supervisor's letter again and threw it back down on the desk. He continued, "But you can't stay in our school unless you salute. If you refuse, it will be the end of a brilliant career. You'll become an outcast . . . and your learning capacity will be useless. Try to understand that, and don't make a foolish decision. You may go." It was a short and straightforward talk.[9]

Simone made her choice. When the other students gave the Hitler salute, she stood still, arms at her side. Shortly afterward, the school expelled her. Other Jehovah's Witnesses would suffer a much worse fate. Many were eventually sent to the concentration camps.

Life and Death Choices

Another young Jehovah's Witness took a deadly stand. On March 28, 1942, twenty-year-old Wolfgang Kusserow was executed for refusing to serve in the army. On the day before his execution, he wrote a final letter to his family:

> My dear Parents, and my dear brothers and sisters!
>
> One more time I am given the opportunity to write you. Well, now I your third son and brother, shall leave you tomorrow early in the morning. Be not sad, the time will come

Jehovah's Witnesses faced persecution throughout the war. These two concentration camp badges bearing purple triangles were worn by Jehovah's Witnesses.

when we shall all be together again. "Those sowing seed with tears will reap even with a joyful cry" . . . So we confidently look forward to the future.

Dear Papa, I am sorry that I was not allowed to visit you early in December. Exactly one year ago from tomorrow I saw you and Hildegard for the last time. In the meantime I have visited Lenchen. It was a special joy for me to see Mummy once again.

Well, dear Mummy, Annemarie read me your dear letter during her visit . . . It is fine that you are busy in the baking factory (prison), so you are at least in a warm room and you have something to eat. Lenchen is now in the concentration camp.

Dear Annemarie, once more special thanks to you for all your endeavors. May our Lord reward you. I have you all constantly in mind . . . Satan knows that his time is short. Therefore, he tries with all his power to lead [people of good will] astray from God, but he will have no success. We know that our faith will be victorious.

In this faith and this conviction I leave you.

A last greeting from this old world in the hope of seeing you again soon in a New World.

"Your son and brother (signed) Wolfgang."[10]

Loyalty to Hitler

Defying Hitler and the Nazi government had deadly consequences. However, through propaganda and a Nazified Germany, the Nazis

Wolfgang Kusserow was executed on March 28, 1942, for refusing to serve in the German army.

had managed to convince many Germans to help out in the war effort. Irmgard Paul was not yet a teenager when she faced a choice between her loyalty to Hitler and love for her anti-Nazi grandfather. She lived in Berchtesgaden, near Hitler's summer home. She had no contact with Jews or "other enemies of the Reich." Her moment of confrontation began with a school project for the war effort:

Monday mornings each pupil had to weigh in with at least two pounds of used paper and a ball of smoothed-out . . . aluminum foil to help with the war effort. Ingrid [my sister] and I were in fierce competition for the few scraps of foil and paper we could get our hands on in both grandparents' households and had difficulty meeting our quotas. [Mother] reused every available paper bag until it was torn to bits; the scanty newspapers were cut for toilet paper, and grocers would put everything unwrapped into our string bags. One rainy day I had a brainstorm. We were playing in my grandfather's large, [dusty] attic, looking through the trade magazines that he had saved over the years. Suddenly I realized that here, right in front of us, were pounds and pounds of paper gathering dust. . . . I had no doubt that [grandfather] would say yes . . . [I] hurried as fast as I could down the three flights of stairs into [his] workshop. . . . [I asked] his permission to take his old journals to school for the recycling collection. He looked at me as if he had not quite understood my question and then said in a calm, icy tone that not a sliver of any of his magazines would go to support the war of that scoundrel Hitler. Disappointment and something akin to hatred must have shown on my face. How dare he not support the war that we were told everyday was a life-and-death struggle for the German people?

[Then one day] I accepted [my teacher's] invitation to have a special treat of hot

85

chocolate and cookies at her house. . . .
I wondered why she had invited me. After
a few [polite words] she asked point-blank
what my grandfather thought about Adolf
Hitler and what he said about the war.
I was still angry with my grandfather
but stalled . . . weighing my feelings
against my answer. On the one hand,
[Grandfather] was withholding paper for
the war effort. . . . On the other hand,
he was my grand-father.

 After much too long a pause I [decided]
that I liked this nosy teacher less than my
grandfather. . . . [I said] that I did not
know what he thought and that he never said
much anyway. . . . and I assured her that
he said nothing about the Führer. . . .
Although I did not know it that day,
[the teacher] was a Nazi informer, and
my telling the truth would have sent [my
grandfather] to a concentration camp.[11]

Some young people made a different choice. Alfons Heck was
thoroughly devoted to the Führer. He entered the Hitler Youth at
the age of ten and worked his way through the ranks, becoming a
senior leader by the time he was sixteen. He confronted his own
demons after the July 20, 1944, attempt to assassinate Adolf
Hitler:

I had no mercy with the plotters. They were
heinous criminals trying to stab [Germany]
in the back. . . . I learned only after the
war that my own father had been detained
overnight by the *Gestapo* [secret police]
early in September and questioned about

his connections to prominent former Social Democrats. . . . He [did not] tell the *Gestapo* that he had fathered me, a leader of the Hitler Youth. If the *Gestapo* had found him involved in the slightest anti-Nazi activity, my status as a loyal adherent to the regime wouldn't have saved him. Despite our opposing views of Nazism, I did not want to see my father come to harm; but if he had plotted against Hitler I would have stopped him. Would I have sent my own father to a concentration camp and likely death? It's conceivable, although I like to think I would have given him one warning before calling the *Gestapo*.[12]

> "Would I have sent my own father to a concentration camp and likely death? It's conceivable, although I like to think I would have given him one warning . . . "

Life Unworthy of Life

Another part of the Nazi plan for a "master race" was killing people with hereditary disabilities, such as mental illness, physical deformity, epilepsy, blindness, and deafness. This began with a forced sterilization law enacted on July 14, 1933. However, the sterilization law was a forerunner for the so-called "euthanasia killings" that began in October 1939. Hitler issued a firm decree empowering physicians to grant "mercy deaths" to "patients considered incurable."[13] Fearful of public reaction, the Nazi regime carried out these killings of patients in mental asylums and other institutions in secret. However, Germans heard many rumors. Irmgard Paul remembered overhearing a conversation about a neighbor girl who disappeared:

> One afternoon . . . Tante [Aunt] Susi and
> my mother talked quietly with serious,
> worried faces. I loved to listen to grown-
> up gossip and moved closer to hear what the
> two women were saying. "One of the Dehmel
> children, the [mentally retarded] one
> that's never outside, was picked up by the
> Health Service a few weeks ago, and now
> they've said she's dead from a cold," said
> my mother. Tante Susi with her pretty
> bobbed haircut shook her head. . . . "Well,
> it's probably true, her dying from a cold,
> I mean" . . . I began to pick some white,
> pink-rimmed daisies as I mulled things
> over. Just that morning I had played with
> [the other Dehmel children] and I knew
> they were fine. I began to wonder about the
> sister who had never played outside. What
> did it mean, she was taken away? She died
> from a cold? Would they take me away if
> I had a cold, and would I die too? I was
> infected by the feeling of unease I had
> sensed during the two women's conversation
> but, as quickly as they had, convinced
> myself that there was nothing to fear.
> Certainly Mutti and Vati [Mama and Papa]
> would never let anyone take me away.
>   What I did not know, and what the adults
> refused to believe or face, was that
> Hitler's [killing] program, while still . . .
> hidden from the general public, was up and
> running. And if Mutti had . . . suspected

Täglich RM 5.50 kostet den Staat ein Erbkranker

Für RM 5.50 kann eine erbgesunde Familie 1 Tag leben !

The Nazi plan for a "master race" also attacked people with hereditary diseases. This propaganda slide produced by the Reich Propaganda Office compares the cost of feeding one person with a hereditary disease to an entire family of healthy Germans.

foul play concerning the Dehmel baby, she would have convinced herself that Hitler himself would not condone such murder.[14]

The drive to Nazify the German nation and purify the Aryan race turned German society upside down. It forced Germans of all ages, races, and religions to deal with Nazism in one way or another. Those who lacked enthusiasm for the Führer and his empire often ended up in concentration camps. Political enemies of the Nazis—communists and socialists—were put in camps. After Kristallnacht, the Nazis deported Jews to concentration camps in Germany.

Irmgard Paul remembered when the brother of her honorary aunt came to visit:

> We knew that [Ferdi] had just been released from Buchenwald, a new kind of prison called K.Z. . . . concentration camp. Tante Susi was visibly shaken on seeing how old and diminished he looked. . . . I realized that the concentration camp was the worst thing that could happen to a person and decided I would never get into the kind of trouble that would send me there.[15]

Regardless of who they were or how they coped, the young people of Germany had to make difficult choices.

Chapter Six

THE HITLER YOUTH

Youth organizations played an important role in Hitler's Germany. The Hitler Youth developed alongside the Nazi Party. It grew in importance after Hitler appointed Baldur von Schirach as Youth Leader of the German Reich in June 1933. To further the development of Hitler Youth groups, the Nazi party outlawed all other organizations for young people, including any church-sponsored programs and sports leagues. Non-Nazi youth organizations disbanded or went underground.

There was the Hitler Youth for boys and the League of German Girls for girls, both divided into subunits based on age. In the beginning, membership was optional. The Hitler Youth Law of December 1936 forced all "Aryan" young people between the ages of fourteen and eighteen to join. Less than three years later, children had to join at the age of ten.

Great Expectations

Alfons Heck joined before membership became compulsory. Writing as an adult, he remembered looking forward to it:

> Far from being forced to enter the ranks of the *Jungvolk* [junior branch of the Hitler Youth], I could barely contain my impatience and was, in fact, accepted before I was quite 10. It seemed like an exciting life, free from parental supervision,

filled with "duties" that seemed sheer
pleasure. Precision marching was something
one could endure for hiking, camping, war
games in the field, and a constant emphasis
on sports. . . . There were the paraphernalia
and the symbols, the pomp and the mysti-
cism, very close in feeling to religious
rituals. One of the first significant
demands was the so-called *Mutprobe*: "test
of courage," which was usually administered

Hitler Youth groups march down the streets of Nuremberg, Germany, in 1933. Baldur von Schirach (at right), leader of the Hitler Youth, salutes the parade marchers.

after a six-month period of probation. The members of my *Schar*, a platoon-like unit of about 40–50 boys, were required to dive off the three-meter board—about 10 feet high—head first into the town's swimming pool. There were some stinging belly flops,

but the pain was worth it when our
Fahnleinfuhrer, the 15-year-old leader of
our *Fahnlein* (literally "little flag"), a
company-like unit of about 160 boys, handed
us the coveted dagger with its inscription
Blood and Honor. From that moment on we
were fully accepted.[1]

Long after the war, Alfons Heck looked back on those days
and realized what it had cost him:

In Hitler's Germany, my Germany, childhood
ended at the age of 10, with admission to
the *Jungvolk*. Thereafter we children became
the political soldiers of the Third Reich.
. . . Unless [children] have singularly
aware parents, the very young become
defenseless receptacles for whatever is
crammed into them.
We, who had never
heard the bracing
tones of dissent,
never doubted for a
moment that we were
fortunate to live in
a country of such
glowing hopes. . . . And unless one was
Jewish, a gypsy, a homosexual or a political opponent of Nazism, the Germany of the
'30s had indeed become a land of promise.[2]

> "In Hitler's Germany . . . childhood ended at the age of 10, with admission to the *Jungvolk*."

To take their place in this land of promise, children like Alfons
Heck took an oath, learned a pledge of allegiance, and recited
Nazi prayers:

The oath: In the presence of this blood

banner which represents our Führer, I
swear to devote all my energies and my
strength to the saviour of our country,
Adolf Hitler. I am willing and ready to
give up my life for him, so help me God.

The pledge of allegiance: I promise to do
my duty in love and loyalty to the Führer
and our flag.

A prayer: Adolf Hitler, you are our great
Führer. Thy name makes the enemy tremble.
Thy Third Reich comes, thy will alone is
law upon the earth. Let us hear daily thy
voice and order us by thy leadership, for
we will obey to the end and even with our
lives. We Praise thee! Heil Hitler![3]

Dogma and ritual worked together with near-constant activity to ensure that the Hitler Youth would play a dominant role in the life of every member. In 1938, an anonymous writer kept track of a typical day in a Hitler Youth camp:

4:45 Am get up. 4:50 gymnastics. 5:15 wash,
make beds. 5:30 coffee break. 5:50 parade.
6:00 march to building site. Work until
14:30 with 30 minute break for breakfast.
15:30–18:00 drill. 18:10–18:45 instruction.
18:45–19:15 cleaning and mending. 19:15
parade. 19:30 announcements. 19:45 supper.
20:00–21:30 singsong or other leisure
activities. 22:00 lights out.[4]

Even at home, the Hitler Youth demanded a great deal of its members, often taking time away from schoolwork and family obligations. Pressed by these demands, Jurgen Herbst could not keep up:

> [My] report cards in school began to reveal that I had entered on a slowly but steadily descending path. By Easter 1940 my overall grade was still "good"; a year later it had dropped to "almost good." Thereafter my teachers continued to [say] that I had begun to slack off. Nevertheless, though I had also shown tendencies to become "disruptive," I still achieved "satisfying results." . . .
>
> The . . . [main] cause of my academic decline was my growing involvement in the [Hitler Youth]. As I passed my fourteenth birthday, I advanced in the ranks step by step from being responsible for a *Jugenschaft* of ten to heading a *Jungvolk* of thirty and finally, as I turned sixteen . . . to command a *Fähnlein* of a hundred.[5]

The League of German Girls

Girls also marched and drilled. They played sports and received regular indoctrination in Nazi principles. Some girls tried to avoid joining; others, like Irmgard Paul, looked forward to it:

> I was now completely focused on joining the Hitler Youth. . . . I would be ten in May— far too old for *Kindergruppe*, I felt—and began to badger Mutti to ask Frau Deil if I could join the Jungmädel, the junior division of the female [Hitler Youth], that would lead me at age fourteen, to enrollment in the BDM (Bund Deutscher Mädchen), the next

Members of the German League of Girls wave Nazi flags in Vienna, Austria, in 1938. Girls marched and drilled and also played sports.

level of a girl's training and indoctrination. Yes, I knew I was the youngest in my grade, and yes, we were late with the application, but how could I tolerate it if all my friends were strutting around in their uniforms every Friday afternoon and I was left out?. . . . Indeed, Frau Deil arranged for my entry.

At our first *Appell* (drill and meeting) we were lined up by size four rows deep and called to order for learning how to march in place. . . . Finally, we . . . marched through town from one end to the other. . . .

I was completely seduced by a feeling of belonging, of being united with all young Germans wearing this uniform. . . .

In addition to marching drills we Jungmädel trained for sports competition, hiked, sang a great deal, and listened to many lectures and speeches by senior leaders. They always said that every boy and girl had to do his or her share to win the war and that we must believe that the Führer was invincible and Germany's only salvation. No one asked a question; it was not called for and we were much too well indoctrinated to do so.[6]

Life on the Fringe

Not all young people got caught up in the Hitler Youth. Some rebelled against its regimentation, and some fought its racism. Jews and other non-Aryan children did not face these choices; they were not allowed to join in the first place. Carola Stern Steinhardt and other Jewish girls did not understand why they were excluded:

We were little kids [and when we saw] . . . a circle of German girls who had these nice outings, we felt so why can't we be part of it. Why can't we be part of it? Why can't we? As a matter of fact, I remember at one point when . . . everybody said, "Heil Hitler" . . . I did, too. What did I know? I was eight years old. So my mother said to me, "You're not supposed to do that." I said, "Why not?" She said, "Haven't you been told that you are Jewish?" I said, "Oh, I forgot." So it was very hard to comprehend. I couldn't get it together that I was suddenly Jewish and I couldn't do whatever I did before.[7]

> "I couldn't get it together that I was suddenly Jewish and I couldn't do whatever I did before."

For Hans Massaquoi, being excluded was even more of a shock. As part of a contest to see which class could enroll 100 percent of its students, the teacher drew a chart of the classroom, with a box for each student:

Each morning, Herr Schürmann would [ask] who had joined the Hitler Youth . . . then gleefully add the new enlistees' names to his chart.

One morning, when the empty squares had dwindled to just a few, Herr Schürmann started querying the holdouts as to their reasons for their "lack of love for Führer and *Vaterland* [Fatherland]." Some explained that they had nothing against Führer

and *Vaterland* but weren't particularly
interested in the kinds of things the
Jungvolk were doing, such as camping,
marching, blowing bugles and fanfares,
and beating on medieval-style drums. . . .
When it came to what I thought was my turn
to explain, I opened my mouth, but Herr
Schürmann cut me off. "That's all right;
you are exempted from the contest since you
are ineligible to join the *Jungvolk*."

The teacher's words struck me like a bolt
of lightning. Not eligible to join? What
was he talking about? I had been prepared
to tell him that I hadn't quite made up my
mind whether I wanted to join or not. Now
he was telling me that, even if I wanted to
I couldn't.[8]

After class, the teacher explained that only pureblooded
"Aryans" could join the Hitler Youth. Hans did not qualify because
his father was African.

The Rebels

Many "Aryan" young people rejected the regimentation of the
Hitler Youth; the uniforms, the endless marching, the pressure to
conform to Nazi ideals. In the 1930s, some of these rebels created
loosely organized groups, such as the Edelweiss Pirates and Swing
Youth, or more informally, the Swing Kids. In general, the Pirates
came from working-class backgrounds while most Swing Kids
belonged to the upper-middle class.

Instead of marching in lockstep with the Hitler Youth, these
sons and daughters of wealth and privilege liked to dress up in
party clothes and dance the night away to American jazz and big

band music. They were not political; they simply rejected the drab conformity of Nazi youth culture.

They also enjoyed shocking that culture. One unnamed Hitler Youth left a record of his reaction:

> The sight of some three hundred dancing
> people thrashing about was absolutely horrid.
> No one can describe the dancing because
> no one danced normally. Indeed, this was
> the naughtiest . . . dancing that can be
> imagined. . . . Everyone jumped about like
> crazy while they mumbled English musical
> gibberish. The Band increased the tempo
> faster by the minute. No member of the band
> was sitting, because they were all getting
> hotter and wilder as they also succumbed
> to the jungle beat on the stage.[9]

By 1941, their loud partying and frenetic jitterbugging had drawn Nazi official attention. On August 18, police arrested more than three hundred Swing Kids. Those identified as leaders found themselves in the concentration camps for "un-German" activities, or

"Everyone jumped about like crazy while they mumbled English musical gibberish."

activities the Nazis did not tolerate. Instead of taming the Swing Kids, this official clampdown made them bolder. They still wanted to have a good time, but they began handing out anti-Nazi literature and viewing their rebellion in another light.

The Edelweiss Pirates were rebels from the beginning. Many of them dropped out of school so they could avoid involvement with both the Nazi Party and the Hitler Youth. They engaged in activities that ranged from mockery of Nazi dogma to malicious mischief and even outright sabotage.

Walter Meyer became part of a Pirate group in the city of Dusseldorf:

> We had [meetings] generally at a cafe on
> . . . Kings Avenue in Dusseldorf [which is]
> one of the best known avenues in the world.
> It's gorgeous, wide, and has a river in the
> middle and all chestnut trees and so on.
> Well there was a cafe and in the back of
> the cafe was a pool room. . . . we used to
> play pool, and we had our little meetings
> there and . . . maybe one would say, "You
> know, the Hitler Youths . . . store their
> . . . equipment at such-and-such a place.
> Let's make it disappear." "Okay, when are
> we going to meet?" Such-and-such a time.
> And that's what we did. It . . . came to
> the point where people began to look for
> us because we went a little too [far] . . .
> you know we started maybe by deflating
> the tires, then we made the whole bicycle
> disappear, so it came to the point where
> [there were] too many complaints.[10]

The Pirates liked to make up their own words to Hitler Youth marching songs, a practice that infuriated the powers-that-be:

> We all sat in the tavern
> With a pipe and a glass of wine,
> A goodly drop of malt and hop,
> And the devil calls the tune.
> * Hark the hearty fellows sing!
> Strum that banjo, pluck that string!
> And the lasses all join in.

```
          We're going to get rid of Hitler,
            And he can't do a thing. . . .
          *Hitler's power may lay us low,
            And keep us locked in chains,
      But we will smash the chains one day,
                We'll be free again.
          We've got fists and we can fight,
        We've got knives and we'll get them out.
        We want freedom, don't we, boys? . . . .
        Out on the high road, down in the ditch
          There're some Hitler Youth patrolmen,
            and they're getting black as pitch.
      Sorry if it hurts, mates, sorry we can't stay,
      We're Edelweiss Pirates, and we're on our way.
      * We march by banks of Ruhr and Rhine [rivers]
            And smash the Hitler Youth in twain,
          Our song is freedom, love and life,
            We're Pirates of the Edelweiss.¹¹
```

The Pirates paid a high price for their activism. After a major roundup in the city of Cologne, the Nazis had thirteen Edelweiss Pirates hanged.

The Crusaders

In the summer of 1942, a small group of students at the University of Munich formed a resistance group called the White Rose. Students Hans and Sophie Scholl, Christoph Probst, Alexander Schmorell, and Willi Graf and Professor Kurt Huber made up the small group. The White Rose published and distributed a series of anti-Nazi pamphlets. The fifth pamphlet, published in February 1943, dared to admit the truth; Germany was losing the war:

```
A Call to All Germans!

The war is approaching its destined end . . .
in the East the [German] armies are
```

constantly in retreat and invasion is [near] in the West. Mobilization in the United States . . . exceeds anything that the world has ever seen. It has become a mathematical certainty that Hitler is leading the German people into the abyss. Hitler cannot win the war; he can only prolong it. The guilt of Hitler and his [followers] goes beyond all measure. Retribution comes closer and closer.

But what are the German people doing? They will not see and will not listen. Blindly they follow their seducers into ruin. Victory at any price! is inscribed on their banner. "I will fight to the last man," says Hitler—but in the meantime the war has already been lost.

Germans! Do you and your children want to suffer the same fate that befell the Jews? . . . Are we to be forever a nation which is hated and rejected by all mankind? No. [Turn away] from National Socialist [Nazi] gangsters. Prove by your deeds that you think otherwise. . . . Cast off the cloak of indifference you have wrapped around you. Make the decision before it is too late. . . . Do not believe that Germany's welfare is linked to the victory of National Socialism for good or ill. A criminal regime cannot achieve a German victory. Separate yourselves in time from everything connected with National Socialism. In the aftermath a terrible but just judgment will be meted out to those who stayed in hiding, who were cowardly and hesitant. . . .

> Freedom of speech, freedom of religion,
> the protection of individual citizens from
> the . . . will of criminal regimes . . .
> will be the [basis] of the New Europe.[12]

While distributing a sixth leaflet, the Scholls were arrested. On February 22, 1943, Hans and Sophie Scholl and Christoph Probst

Sophie Scholl was a member of the White Rose resistance group. This portrait of her was taken sometime in 1941.

were beheaded. Graf, Schmorell, and Professor Huber were later arrested and executed.

The Boy Soldiers

After Germany's defeat at Stalingrad on February 2, 1943, Nazi fortunes plummeted. By the summer of 1943, ten thousand boys younger than age seventeen began training to be soldiers.[13] Older members of the Hitler Youth found themselves called up to the front lines. These inexperienced boy soldiers did not fare well.

> "I saw the horrors that no . . . boy should ever see."

Gerhardt Thamm remembered his mandatory service: "As a fifteen-year-old boy I fought briefly in a war. My fight was neither noble nor heroic. I saw the horrors that no fifteen-year-old boy should ever see. I came into war purely by unfortunate happenstance, and survived it purely by lucky coincidence."[14]

Training was brief and harsh. Gerhardt remembered being pushed to exhaustion during a simple run. After being told again and again to run faster, some of the boys could not keep up:

```
The formation started to stretch out. Some
of the boys at the front faded and the for-
mation began to disintegrate. Finally some
of the boys, white clouds of breath expel-
ling from [their] lungs . . . slowed down
and started to walk. In a flash . . . the
sergeant rushed up and screamed. . . . "Is
this what the Hitler Youth has produced? A
bunch of weaklings? Move it! Move it! . . .
The Führer does not want weaklings! He
wants Father land defenders! You are his
```

last hope. Run!" . . . [Then] he watched as
we, heaving, coughing, [struggled] to make
the last circuit around the parade ground.

As we came out of the last turn [an]
elderly soldier . . . surveyed the
decrepit group and told us to get into
formation. . . . He reminded us that we
were not a bunch of sheep, but German
soldiers, and never to forget it. [Then]
he turned and walked toward the sergeant,
saluted, and [left]. The sergeant . . .
walked totally around the platoon, returned
to front and center, and spoke in an almost
normal human voice. "I will make soldiers
out of you! . . . You may think you are
just a bunch of boys, but when I am through
with you, you will be the most efficient
killing machine the world has ever known—or
you will be dead!"[15]

No one knows exactly how many boys died in combat, but there are statistics about particular units in certain battles. For example, of the ten thousand boys in Gerhardt Thamm's unit, only six hundred survived.[16] In April 1945, a unit of five thousand boys tried to defend the Pichelsdorf bridges into Berlin. Over a period of five days, all but five hundred boys were killed or wounded.[17] Like other survivors, these boy soldiers were left to face what their nation had become in pursuit of an evil dream.

Chapter Seven

COMING TO THE END

In the beginning, dealing with what Hitler called "the Jewish problem" did not include killing all the Jews in Europe. However, then came the ghettos and concentration camps of Poland and the killing squads that slaughtered entire communities of Soviet Jews. In January 1942, a group of high-ranking Nazis gathered in the resort town of Wannsee, Germany. There, they established control over the implementation of the plan to murder all the Jews in Europe. They called it the "final solution" to the Jewish problem.

A year later the war turned against Germany as Soviet troops crushed the German Sixth Army at Stalingrad. Many Nazi leaders took this as the beginning of the end for Hitler's Thousand Year Reich. They dared not voice this opinion, though; to do so would be treason. While the war effort faltered, the destruction of the European Jews picked up pace. Gas chambers that looked like shower rooms but dispensed poison gas rather than water operated day and night in the death camps; crematoria, or brick ovens for burning bodies, spewed dark smoke into the air. The smell of death spread everywhere.

Taken Away

When it became obvious to many Germans that the war remained hopeless, the Nazis stepped up their program for killing the Jews.

The authorities sent German Jews to ghettos and annihilation camps in Poland, where many were immediately gassed. Those who were spared for slave labor knew that any moment could be their last.

In 1944, teenager Cecilia Landau was deported from Germany to the Auschwitz death camp in Poland. There, she faced the awful horrors of selections in which SS officers chose who would live and who would die:

> One evening, shortly after our arrival, Maja [the prisoner in charge of the barracks] announced that . . . Dr. Mengele would inspect the prisoners. "The procedure is simple," she said. "You take off your dress, carry it in the left hand, and walk naked past the SS inspection team. Be fast and don't talk. They'll decide."
>
> "Decide what?" I whispered to Elli [a friend].
>
> "I've heard rumors that Mengele selects some for work, some for hospital experiments, and some for the gas chambers," Elli whispered in response. Once again, the SS would determine life and death. . . .
>
> Morning broke, gray and dismal, and again we lined up, Elli and I still together. We stood and waited, our scantily clad bodies shivering. Three SS officers suddenly marched into the center of the [compound]. . . .
>
> "The one with the baton is Mengele," someone whispered. "He is God here. He'll sentence us—to work, to the gas chambers, or the hospital."

Maja now faced us. "Achtung! Remove dresses! Carry them in your left hand. First row, march—fast! Don't dally!"

Those in front of us almost ran past the three SS officers, while Mengele appraised them like cattle, motioning—right, left, right, left.

His face was expressionless, almost casual.

"Next row!"

Elli nudged me, whispering, "Walk fast. Don't look at anyone."

Shamefully, I began running naked across the field, forcing myself not to think. Dress in hand, I stumbled past the Germans, who stood no more than three feet away. I raced on, avoiding their stares, but out of the corner of my eye I saw the swinging baton in Mengele's hand motion me to the right. Was right better than left? Elli followed close behind and was also signaled to the right. Realizing that we were still together, we breathed a sigh of relief. At least half of the group has been directed to the left and were already being led away. We soon lost sight of them.[1]

Freedom!

The people on the left most likely went straight to the gas chambers. The very old, the very young, and the obviously sick or crippled were usually selected for immediate death. Those who looked like they could work might be saved for a time. As the German army crumbled before the Allied advance, the trains kept running and the death camps kept killing. However, troops from

A group of elderly Jewish men from Subcarpathian Rus (present-day Ukraine) are walking to the gas chambers in Auschwitz after being selected for death. Cecilia Landau faced the selections in Auschwitz in 1944, but she was not chosen for immediate death.

the United States, Great Britain, and the Soviet Union (known in World War II as the Allies) began liberating concentration camps one by one. Many inmates were too sick for help; they died with freedom at hand. The survivors were both stunned and puzzled by this sudden liberty.

At the Woebbelin camp in Germany, teenager George Salton barely realized what was happening:

> [As] I came onto that place I noticed many prisoners yelling and screaming and jumping and dancing. And there standing amongst them were seven giants, young people. They must have been 18 or 19 . . . American soldiers. There were seven or eight of them standing inside the camp. Apparently they cut the wire and came into the camp. They were bewildered by us. Wild and unkempt and dirty and, I'm sure, smelly people, jumping and dancing and trying to embrace them and kiss them. And I did too. I also joined the crowd and yelled and screamed and somehow knew that the day of liberation [had] come. It was a strange feeling for me, however, because as I remember it . . . I was overwhelmed by this unexpected and unhoped for encounter of freedom, but at the same time, what was happening was outside of me. I really . . . I didn't know what to make of it. I knew I was free, but I didn't count on it. I somehow didn't know what it meant. And I knew it was great, but . . . I was overjoyed because all people around me were overjoyed and were singing and dancing . . . [but] I was 17. . . . I was free, but what it meant I wasn't sure.[2]

Three young survivors pose smiling for their American liberators in the Buchenwald concentration camp. The reign of Hitler and the Nazis, which ended in 1945, forever changed the lives of young people in Germany and throughout Europe.

Nobody in Hitler's Germany escaped unchanged after twelve years of Nazi rule. Jews and other non-Aryans carried nightmarish memories that would be with them for the rest of their lives. For Jewish young people, those memories included a childhood forever shattered by hatred, and the knowledge that lost innocence could never be reclaimed.

TIMELINE

January 30, 1933—Adolf Hitler becomes chancellor of Germany.

April 25, 1933—Law Against the Crowding of German Schools and Institutions of Higher Learning restricts the number of Jewish students allowed to attend.

May 10, 1933—More than twenty thousand "un-German" books are burned in Munich.

August 2, 1934—President Paul von Hindenburg dies; Adolf Hitler declares himself both president and chancellor of Germany.

September 15, 1935—The Nuremberg Laws deprive Jews of German citizenship.

November 7, 1938—Herschel Grynszpan shoots a German Embassy official in Paris.

November 9–10, 1938—*Kristallnacht*, nationwide violence against Jews in Germany, follows the death of the embassy official.

November 15, 1938—Jewish students are formally expelled from German schools. They must attend only Jewish schools.

December 2–3, 1938—Jews are banned from streets on certain days and denied drivers' licenses and car registrations.

December 3, 1938—Jewish teachers and students are banned from German universities.

March 22, 1941—Gypsy and African-German students are banned from German schools.

June 1942—The German government closes all Jewish schools.

April 30, 1945—Adolf Hitler commits suicide.

May 7, 1945—Germany surrenders, ending World War II in Europe.

CHAPTER NOTES

Chapter 1. The Teenage Assassin

1. Gerald Schwab, *The Day the Holocaust Began: The Odyssey of Herschel Grynszpan* (Westport, Conn.: Praeger Publishers, 1990), p. 2.
2. "Kristallnacht," *The History Place: World War II in Europe*, 1996, <http://www.historyplace.com/worldwar2/timeline/knacht.htm> (October 9, 2008).

Chapter 2. The Nazi Racial State Begins

1. Dennis Showalter and William J. Astore, *Hindenburg: Icon of German Militarism* (Washington, D.C.: Potomac Books, 2005), p. 92.
2. Melita Maschmann, *Account Rendered: A Dossier on My Former Self* (London: Abelard-Schumann, 1965), pp. 11–12.
3. Ezra BenGershôm, *David: Testimony of a Holocaust Survivor* (Oxford: Berg Publishers Limited, 1988), pp. 22–23.
4. Hans J. Massaquoi, *Destined to Witness: Growing Up Black in Nazi Germany* (New York: William Morrow and Company, 1999), pp. 43–45.
5. Willy Schumann, *Being Present: Growing Up in Hitler's Germany* (Kent, Ohio: Kent State University Press, 1991), p. 27.
6. Elizabeth Kaufmann Koenig, United States Holocaust Memorial Museum (USHMM) *Oral History Interview*, RG-50.030*111.
7. Edith Gerda Reimer, USHMM *Survivor Testimonies*, RG-01.036.
8. Lore Metzger, USHMM Archives, RG-02.018.
9. Carola Stern Steinhardt, USHMM *Survivor Testimonies*, RG-50.030*0368.
10. Interview with Walter F., San Francisco: Holocaust Oral History Project, May 15, 1990, <http://remember.org/witness/wit.sur.franck.html> (December 12, 2008).
11. Alfred Feldman, *One Step Ahead: A Jewish Fugitive in Hitler's Europe* (Carbondale, Ill.: Southern Illinois University Press, 2001), pp. 4–5.

Chapter 3. Who Is a Jew?

1. Henry Landman, USHMM *Survivors Testimonies*, Archives 1997.A.0175.
2. "The Reich Citizenship Law of September 15, 1935, and the First Regulation to the Reich Citizenship Law of November 14, 1935," United States Chief Counsel for the Prosecution of Axis Criminality, *Nazi*

Conspiracy and Aggression, Volume IV (Washington, D.C.: United States Government Printing Office, 1946), Documents 1416-PS and 1417-PS, pp. 7–10.

3. Dora Kramen Dimitro, USHMM *Oral History Interview*, RG 50.030-0372.

4. "Regulation Requiring Jews to Change Their Names, August 1938," Yad Vashem: The Holocaust Martyrs' and Heroes' Remembrance Authority, 2004, <http://www1.yadvashem.org/about_holocaust/documents/part1/doc46.html> (December 12, 2008).

5. Interview of Guy Stern, USHMM, RG-50.030*-223.

6. Eve Nussbaum Soumerai, *A Voice From the Holocaust* (Westport, Conn.: Greenwood Press, 2003), pp. 43–44.

7. Edith Gerder Reimer, USHMM *Survivor Testimonies*, Autobiography, RG-01.036.

8. Magda Lipner, USHMM *Survivor Testimonies*, RG-02.205.

9. Ernest Günter Fontheim, "A Personal Memoir of 'Kristallnacht,'" *Aufbau*, No. 26, December 18, 1998, haGalil.com, 1995–2006, <http://www.hagalil.com/deutschland/berlin/gemeinde/fontheim.htm> (December 16, 2008).

10. Y. S. Herz, "*Kristallnacht* at the Dinslaken Orphanage," *Yad Vashem Studies*, Vol. XI, 1976, pp. 345–349.

11. Fred Ederer, USHMM *Survivor Testimonies*, RG-01.087.

12. Soumerai, p. 15.

13. Ibid., pp. 36–37.

14. Ibid., pp. 49–50.

Chapter 4. Jews and Other Non-Aryans at Nazified Schools

1. "Hitler Youth," *The History Place*, n.d., <http://www.historyplace.com/worldwar2/hitleryouth/hj-timeline.htm> (September 28, 2008).

2. Henry Landman, USHMM *Survivors Testimonies*, Archives 1997.A.0175.

3. Simone Arnold Liebster, *Facing the Lion: Memoirs of a Young Girl in Nazi Europe* (New Orleans: Grammaton Press, 2000), p. 223.

4. Interview with Survivor Walter F., San Francisco: Holocaust Oral History Project, May 15, 1990, <http://remember.org/witness/wit.sur.franck.html> (December 12, 2008).

5. Gad Beck, USHMM *Oral History Interview*, RG-50.030*0361.

6. Ezra BenGershôm, *David: Testimony of a Holocaust Survivor* (Oxford: Berg Publishers Limited, 1988), p. 27.

7. Hans J. Massaquoi, *Destined to Witness: Growing Up Black in Hitler's Germany* (New York: William Morrow and Company, 1999), p. xii.

8. Henry Landman, USHMM *Survivors Testimonies*, Archives 1997.A.0175.

9. Elvira Bauer, *Trust No Fox in the Green Meadow and No Jew on His Oath* (Nuremburg: Stürmer Publishing House, 1936), English translation by Edward J. Kunzer, "The Youth of Nazi Germany," *Journal of Educational Sociology*, Vol. 11, No. 6, February 1938, p. 348.

10. BenGershôm, p. 43.

11. Masssaquoi, pp. 67–68.

12. Interview with survivor Walter F., May 15, 1990.

13. Lore Metzger, USHMM Archives, RG 02.018.

14. Klaus Langer, "Diary Entry November 16, 1938," in Alexandra Zapruder, ed., *Salvaged Pages: Young Writers' Diaries of the Holocaust* (New Haven, Conn.: Yale University Press, 2002).

Chapter 5. Gentile Young People: Pressure to Conform

1. "The Hitler Youth," The History Place, n.d., <http://www.historyplace.com/worldwar2/hitleryouth/index.html> (October 4, 2008).

2. James W. Miller, "Youth in Dictatorships," *The American Political Science Review*, vol. 32, no. 5, October 1938, p. 966.

3. Willy Schumann, *Being Present: Growing Up in Hitler's Germany* (Kent, Ohio: Kent State University Press, 1991), p. 40.

4. Ibid., pp. 41–43.

5. Ibid., p. 29.

6. Melita Maschmann, *Account Rendered: A Dossier on My Former Self* (London: Abelard-Schumann, 1965), pp. 40–41.

7. Jurgen Herbst, *Requiem for a German Past: A Boyhood Among the Nazis* (Madison, Wis.: University of Wisconsin Press, 1999), pp. 73–74.

8. Ibid., pp. 64–65.

9. Simone Arnold Liebster, *Facing the Lion: Memoirs of a Young Girl in Nazi Europe* (New Orleans: Grammaton Press, 2000), pp. 179–81.

10. "Last Letter From Wolfgang Kusserow," Kusserow Family Collection, USHMM RG-32.002*01.

11. Irmgard A. Hunt, *On Hitler's Mountain: Overcoming the Legacy of a Nazi Childhood* (New York: Harper Perennial, 2006), p. 155–158.

12. Alfons Heck, *The Burden of Hitler's Legacy* (Phoenix: Renaissance House Publishers, 1988), pp. 106–107.

13. "Mentally and Physically Handicapped: Victims of the Nazi Era," *United States Holocaust Memorial Museum*, n.d., <http://www.ushmm.org/education/resource/handic/handicapped.php?theme=educators> (October 22, 2008).

14. Hunt, pp. 66–67.

15. Ibid., pp. 68–70.

Chapter 6. The Hitler Youth

1. Alfons Heck, *Child of Hitler: Germany in the Days When God Wore a Swastika* (Phoenix: Renaissance House Publishers, 1985), p. 9.

2. Ibid., pp. 1–3.

3. "Hitler Youth: Principles and Ideology," *Historical Boys' Uniforms*, November 4, 2002, <http://histclo.com/youth/youth/org/nat/hitler/prin/hj-prin.htm> (December 17, 2007).

4. J. Noaakes and G. Pridham, eds., *Nazism: A History in Documents and Eyewitness Accounts, 1919–1945, Vol. 1* (New York: Schocken Books, 1983), pp. 480–481.

5. Jurgen Herbst, *Requiem for a German Past: A Boyhood Among the Nazis* (Madison, Wis.: University of Wisconsin Press, 1999), p. 91.

6. Irmgard A. Hunt, *On Hitler's Mountain: Overcoming the Legacy of a Nazi Childhood* (New York: Harper Perennial, 2006), pp. 171–174.

7. Carola Stern Steinhardt, USHMM *Survivor Testimonies*, RG-50.030*0368.

8. Hans J. Massaquoi, *Destined to Witness: Growing Up Black in Hitler's Germany* (New York: William Morrow and Company, 1999), pp. 99–100.

9. "German Swing Youth," *Swingstyle Syndicate*, n.d., <http://www.return2style.de/amiswhei.htm> (September 8, 2008).

10. "German Resistance to Hitler: Walter Meyer," United States Holocaust Memorial Museum, Collections, n.d., <http://www.ushmm.org/wlc/media_oi.php?lang=sp&ModuleId=10005208&MediaId=1236&print=y> (December 12, 2008).

11. Detler J.K. Reukert, *Inside Germany: Conformity, Opposition, and Racism in Everyday Life* (New Haven, Conn.: Yale University Press, 1987), pp. 157–158.

12. "White Rose—Leaflet 5," libcom.org, December 6, 2005, <http://libcom.org/library/white-rose-leaflet-5> (December 12, 2008).

13. "Hitler's Boy Soldiers: 1939–1945," *The History Place*, 1999, <http://www.historyplace.com/worldwar2/hitleryouth/hj-boy-soldiers.htm> (September 29, 2008).

14. Gerhardt B. Thamm, *Boy Soldier: A German Teenager at the Nazi Twilight* (Jefferson, N.C.: McFarland & Company, 1999), p. 2.

15. Ibid., p. 108.

16. "Hitler's Boy Soldiers: 1939–1945."

17. Ibid.

Chapter 7. Coming to the End

1. Lucille Eichengreen, *From Ashes to Life: My Memories of the Holocaust* (San Francisco: Mercury House, 1994), pp. 99–100.

2. "George Salton Describes Liberation by American Soldiers," United States Holocaust Memorial Museum, Liberation of Nazi Camps, n.d., <http://www.ushmm.org/wlc/media_oi.php?lang=en&ModuleId=10005131&MediaId=3279> (December 12, 2008).

GLOSSARY

Aryan—Hitler's name for the Germanic and Nordic "master race."

chancellor—Head of government in a parliamentary system. Carries on the business of government and supervises its various agencies.

concentration camp—A camp for confining political prisoners, enemy aliens, and civilians who ran afoul of the government.

crematorium—Large, super-hot furnace for burning bodies.

"final solution"—The term for the Nazi plan to solve what they called the "Jewish problem" or "Jewish question" by killing all the Jews in Europe.

gas chamber—In Nazi Germany, a sealed room for killing groups of people; often disguised as a shower room.

ghetto—In Nazi Germany, a run-down area in a city or town where Jews were confined.

Holocaust—Literally "to destroy by fire." Name given to the destruction of European Jews during World War II.

indoctrinate—To teach an uncritical acceptance of a particular point of view.

propaganda—A one-sided communication, presenting a single point of view.

Reichstag—German parliament; also, the parliament building.

selection—In Nazi Germany, a sorting-out of people for deportation or death.

visa—Travel papers allowing a person to enter a country.

FURTHER READING

BenGershôm, Ezra. *David: The Testimony of a Holocaust Survivor*. New York: Oswald Wolff Books, 1989.

Boraks-Nemetz, Lilian and Irene N. Watts, eds. *Tapestry of Hope: Holocaust Writing for Young People*. Plattsburg, N.Y.: Tundra Books of Northern New York, 2003.

Chapman, Fern Schumer. *Motherland: Beyond the Holocaust: A Mother-Daughter Journey to Reclaim the Past*. New York: Penguin Books, 2001.

Holliday, Laurel, ed. *Children in the Holocaust and in World War II: Their Secret Diaries*. New York: Washington Square Press, 1996.

Hunt, Irmgard A. *On Hitler's Mountain: Overcoming the Legacy of a Nazi Childhood*. New York: HarperCollins, 2005.

Massaquoi, Hans J. *Destined to Witness: Growing Up Black in Nazi Germany*. New York: William Morrow and Company, 1999.

Rogasky, Barbara. *Smoke and Ashes: The Story of the Holocaust*. New York: Holiday House, 2002.

Strickland, Eycke. *Eyes Are Watching, Ears Are Listening: Growing Up in Nazi Germany 1933–1946*. Lincoln, Nebr.: iUniverse, Inc., 2008.

INTERNET ADDRESSES

United States Holocaust Memorial Museum
   <http://www.ushmm.org/>

USC Shoah Foundation Institute
   <http://college.usc.edu/vhi/>

Yad Vashem, The Holocaust Martyrs' and Heroes' Remembrance
   Authority
   <http://www.yadvashem.org/>

INDEX

A

administrators, replacement of, 63–67

African-Germans, 17–20

antisemitism, learning, 74–78. *See also* education.

"Aryan" race, 13, 30, 36, 60, 89, 91, 100

Austria, 37

B

Bar Mitzvah, 27

Beck, Gad, 57–58

BenGershôm, Ezra, 15–17, 58–59, 63

book burnings, 50, 60

C

citizenship, loss of, 30–32

concentration camps
    internment of Jews in, 10, 45, 48
    liberation of, 110–114
    as penalty, 89–90, 101

crematoria, 108

Czechoslovakia, 37–38

D

death camps, 108–110

Dimitro, Dora Kramen, 33

Dinslaken orphanage, 42–45

E

Edelweiss Pirates, 100–103

education

banning of Jews from, 67–69

curriculum changes, 59–62, 70–71

discrimination in, 23

Nazification in, 53–59

euthanasia killings, 87–90

executions, 81–83, 105–106

F

Feldman, Alfred, 27–29

"final solution," 108–110

Fontheim, Ernest, 38–42

G

gas chambers, 108, 110

genocide, 13

Gestapo, 27, 34–36, 86–87

Goebbels, Joseph, 9

Graf, Willi, 103, 106

Grynszpan, Herschel, 7–12, 38

H

Heck, Alfons, 86–87, 91–95

Herbst, Jurgen, 75–79, 96

Hertz, Y. S., 42–45

Heydrich, Reinhard, 9–10

Hindenburg, Paul von, 13, 29

Hitler, Adolf
    appointment as Chancellor, 13–17
    assassination plot against, 86–87
    persecution of Jews by. *See* Jews, persecution of.
    political philosophy of, 13–14, 53, 70